Thinking of...

Digital Transformation from the Board's Perspective?

Ask the Smart Questions

By Stephen Parker & David Cleminson

Smart Questions™ Philosophy

Smart Questions is built on 3 key pillars, which set it apart from other publishers:

1. *Smart people want Smart Questions not Dumb Answers*
2. *Domain experts are often excluded from authorship, so we are making writing a book simple and painless*
3. *The community has a great deal to contribute to enhance the content*

www.smart-questions.com

COVID-19

We had effectively completed this book just before the arrival of the COVID-19 pandemic. Like most people, we assumed/hoped that it would all be over soon, and we would just delay publication by a few weeks. However, as we now know, this was not the case and the personal and economic impacts have been felt globally.

> **Our thoughts go out to anyone who has been impacted, either directly or indirectly, by COVID-19.**

We considered whether to update the book with specific COVID-19 references in each chapter and additional COVID-19 specific questions. However, after several long discussions we decided that we did not want this book to be locked into the COVID moment and become "Digital Transformation in COVID-19 times".

Additionally, after a detailed review, we felt that the existing content already provided sufficient coverage for the concept of "disruptive transformation" and that the content would be relevant, not just for COVID-19, but for any other unknown/unknown scenarios. The message of being prepared for change even when you are at the top of your game, is already a key theme of the book.

What COVID-19 has done, has highlighted the need for adaptability and flexibility, especially for those who may have been reluctant to change, or may not have seen how change was relevant to them. In this context COVID-19 has clearly acted as an accelerator by creating urgency and removing many of the possible choices. Also, COVID-19 has meant that some of the barriers to change, that were previously in the "too hard bucket", have become "just fix it now or we cannot operate" decisions.

For example, staff working from home has previously raised many legitimate concerns for companies:

- Is the employee home a safe place to work?
- How do we manage company assets that leave the office?
- How do we monitor working hours and practices?
- etc etc.

Whilst these questions are still valid, COVID-19 has altered the risk/reward balance and the reality for many companies has been "We had no choice and in fact we are pleasantly surprised by the reality." For many employees there may also be a reluctance to return to the "old ways" and hence ongoing transformation will be required.

So, in conclusion:

- This book was always about sharing the Smart Questions that will help Directors prepare their companies for disruption and transformation
- Whilst COVID-19 is an EXTREEM case it is within the context of the book as originally envisioned
- Even in these COVID times, the content is valid and therefore, there is no need for a re-write.

Stephen and David

Foreword

The rate of business and environmental change is increasing to unprecedented levels, resulting in organisations having to constantly respond to both opportunities and threats. In my industry for example this include area such as:

- Deregulated markets
- A move away from a government funded allocation paradigm
- A move towards a competitive market paradigm which sees increased customer choice and stronger competition

As Directors and executives, we are all endeavouring to ensure that our organisations are strategically positioned to maximise opportunities as they arise, as well as effectively managing significant future disruption.

In my various roles, one as an executive and the other as a Board Director, it is my objective to ensure, from a strategic perspective, I understand the key and 'fresh' questions I need to ask in order to perform each of these roles appropriately by adopting a different lenses when reviewing strategy.

The first two Chapters of this book cover various aspects of transformation, disruption and change management as well as more importantly, providing clarification of the terms, Digital and Business Transformation. I believe for many people there is confusion about these terms and they are often used interchangeably when referring to different aspects of transformation. The examples provided offer a good insight into how organisations have understood and employed critical technology and key business drivers to maximise opportunities and bring disruption to the market.

Chapters Five through Seven are a 'breath of fresh air'. They provide in an easy to read format, realistic insights into the questions to be asked from an internal, external, and technological perspective.

The introduction of the concept of 3 'R's being reinforce, remind and reveal, provide a relevant prompt for readers to review previous or new insights. The thinking that underpins the suggested questions allows readers to gain a better understanding of the crux of many of the problems requiring resolution.

In summary, a very good read which is highly recommended for executives and board directors, who are developing and responding to rapid change through strategy, within this current challenging and transformational environment (i.e. all of us).

Dione O'Donnell MBA GAICD
Executive Director Corporate Services, Mayflower Brighton
Board Director – Windana Drug & Alcohol Ltd

Authors

Stephen Parker (GAICD, MACS Snr CP)

A translator between Directors, CxO's and IT Pros, connecting Digital Transformation to Business Transformation.

With over 30 years of business transformation experience, Stephen provides creative and challenging thinking that aligns essential business needs with innovative technology.

He has gained experience in executive leadership roles (from start-ups to multinationals), working closely with leading software vendors on their global cloud strategy, providing associate services to industry analysts, sharing knowledge as a keynote speaker and university lecturer, offering independent consulting services and writing a variety of books covering the technology space.

(*www.linkedin.com/in/sjkparker*)

David Cleminson (GAICD)

David has been working in the Digital technology & Cloud landscape, across multiple industries for the last 25+ Years. His passion is looking at these opportunities and challenges from different perspectives. It's about how businesses can leverage off digital technology to achieve results in a shorter, more straightforward and more efficient manner. How digital technology can simplify and facilitate enablers to provide more capabilities; and deliver higher value.

With 25+ years in the Digital Technology, Cloud, Solution and Technical Integration landscapes, David has been a forward thinking Entrepreneur, Innovator, Author and Facilitator for solving business problems with technology. He is also a graduate of the AICD and an affiliate member of the IoTAA (Smart Cities & Industry and Network & Security Streams)

A primary role in his strategy is "Bridging the gap between the Board and the Digital Landscape".

Table of Contents

Acknowledgements

This book has been driven by our desire to share the experiences we have gained over many years of aligning business value with innovative technologies (don't be fooled by our youthful looks!!).

So, our thanks go out to all the people who have been part of that journey. We have worked as co-workers with some of you and as business partners with others. The ways you have helped us learn and motivated us have been many and varied. Some were positive and enjoyable, whilst others, if we are honest, we would not choose to repeat.

However, all these experiences have provided us with the knowledge that allows us to share the "smart questions" today and for that....

WE THANK YOU ALL

Who should read this book?

Books can be read by many people who will each take away their version of the story. However, as authors, it is essential that we identify a primary audience. This ensures there is clarity in the message we are trying to communicate and a voice that is appropriate.

Primary Audience – Directors and Executives as Problem Shapers

If you are a Director or executive of a medium to large organisation that is thinking about what Digital Transformation means to your business, then this book is aimed at you.

In writing this book, our goal has been to put ourselves in the shoes of Directors and consider the potentially profound impact that Digital Transformation could have on the future of the business. Importantly, we are asking the smart questions that will help in "Problem shaping" not "Problem solving", with a lens of strategy development, policy making, supervision and external accountability (Robert Tricker – Corporate Governance[1]).

What do we mean by "Director"?

The term "Director" can have different meanings in a business context. We want to be clear that in the context of this book we are defining Director as:

> "A member of the governing board of a business concern who may or may not have an executive function" (Collins Dictionary)

In this context, Directors have legal responsibilities defined in a specific jurisdictions company laws (for example The Australian Corporations Act 2001[2] and the UK Companies Act 2006[3])

---

[1] *http://www.bobtricker.co.uk/corporate-governance.html*
[2] *https://www.legislation.gov.au/Details/C2012C00275*
[3] *http://www.legislation.gov.uk/ukpga/2006/46/pdfs/ukpga_20060046_en.pdf*

Secondary Audience – Executives and Managers as Problem Solvers

Understanding the questions that a Director is thinking about when they are "Problem shaping", will make it easier for our secondary "Problem solving" audience of executives and managers as they position their thinking, actions, and proposals.

So, whether you are:

- The executive team reporting to the Board of Directors
- An Enterprise Architect reporting to the Board of Directors and executives
- An internal project manager responsible for digital transformation projects
- An Outsourced Service provider
- Any other digital "Problem solver."

We trust you will also find this book useful.

How to use this book

This book is intended to be a catalyst for action. We have structured the book in what we trust is an easy to follow format:

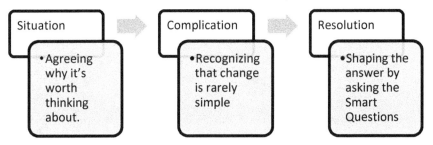

Figure 1 - How to use this book

The first two sections (Situation and Complication) are about setting the scene. In the resolution section, we share the Smart Questions that we trust will assist in "problem shaping" the Digital Transformation opportunity for your organisation.

While we believe this flow has merit, please feel free to start wherever you want. You may be confident enough to jump straight to Chapter 3 and the start of the Smart Questions.

Regardless of the order that you read this book, we hope that the ideas and examples inspire you to act. So, do whatever you need to do to make this book useful. Use Post-it notes, write on it, rip it apart, or scan it in one sitting. We hope this becomes your most dog-eared book.

Chapter

Transformation as an Opportunity

The future is already here – it just isn't very evenly distributed

William Gibson (American-Canadian writer, 1948 –)

D IGITAL Transformation feels like it is the headline in articles across every business sector. Some of these stories present the positive opportunities for growth and efficiency gains, while others discuss disruption, the rise of the robots and negation of whole business models. Of course, hyperbole is natural during the emergence of new ideas and business models. However, what is also true, is that if you allow change **to be forced on you**, then you will have far less control of the outcomes than if you **actively engage in the change process**.

Great business leaders have seen change and transformation as an opportunity rather than a threat and founded businesses that were exemplars both then and now:

- Richard Arkwright[4] - considered the father of the modern industrial factory system. His inventions were a catalyst for the original Industrial Revolution.
- Henry Ford[5] - founder of the Ford Motor Company, and the sponsor of the development of the assembly line technique of mass production.

---

[4] *http://www.bbc.co.uk/history/historic_figures/arkwright_richard.shtml*
[5] *https://en.wikipedia.org/wiki/Henry_Ford*

- Thomas Watson Jr[6] – 2nd CEO of IBM. He recognised the potential of electronics in information handling and drove IBM's transition from punched card tabulators and clocks to transistors and integrated circuits.
- William (Bill) Gates[7] – Co-founder of Microsoft. His vision for personal computing has been central to the success of Microsoft and the wider software industry.
- Jack Ma[8] – Co-founder of Alibaba Group. Recognised the opportunity of the Cloud and aligned this to the growth of the Chinese market. Alibaba has grown from a start-up in 1999 to a USD422Bn global leader (as at 9th August 2019).

If it's not connected to the business, then what's the point.

For all the focus on the word "digital" and the implication that this current transformational opportunity is about technology, the reality is that if solutions are not grounded in valuable business outcomes, then they serve no purpose. It is the intersection of digital transformation and business transformation where true value creation and the potential for disruption lie. Shaping the discussions that lead to this beneficial intersection for the business is a core part of the director's remit.

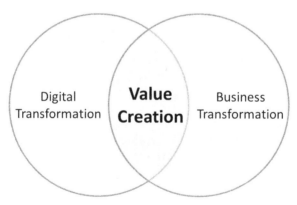

Figure 2 - Value Creation

---

[6] https://www-03.ibm.com/ibm/history/exhibits/watsonjr/watsonjr_intro.html
[7] https://news.microsoft.com/exec/bill-gates/
[8] https://en.wikipedia.org/wiki/Jack_Ma

What is driving this opportunity

We have been living in an increasingly digital world since the 1960's, so what is different about today?

There have been radical enhancements in multiple areas of technology and a fundamental shift in societies engagement with the digital world, that has led us to a tipping point. The WEF (World Economic Forum) has coined the phrase "the fourth industrial revolution" to frame this discussion[9].

> It is characterized by a range of new technologies that are fusing the physical, digital and biological worlds, impacting all disciplines, economies and industries, and even challenging ideas about what it means to be human[10].

The first, second and third industrial revolutions were separated by 80 ~100 years. However, the third is only 50 years old and we are already entering the fourth. The availability of cheap and easy to access technology resources, has created an insatiable drive to develop new solutions that are changing the strategies and priorities of business.

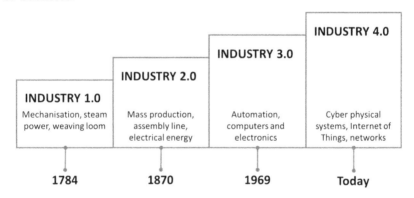

Figure 3 - Industrial Revolutions 1 to 4

That we are discussing the "Fourth" revolution is indicative that these mass changes are not new. While there have been challenges along the way, on balance, society has significantly benefitted from these revolutions and the extreme fears of the "naysayers" have not played out. With each of these "revolutions" we have not just refined what is already in place, we have opened the doors to ideas

---

[9] https://www.weforum.org/agenda/archive/fourth-industrial-revolution
[10] https://www.weforum.org/about/the-fourth-industrial-revolution-by-klaus-schwab

that were initially the figments of some futurologists imagination and turned them into reality.

Technology has enabled the "consumer" to have access to information as never before and through this hold organisations responsible and accountable; not just financially but also morally, socially and ethically. This shift in power from institutions to consumers is forcing companies to change strategic direction and rethink operating models[11].

> Leading companies — and the decisions that they make — will determine the impact that these technologies will have on society[12].

Technology Drivers

Radical change happens where multiple forces interact and complement each other at the same time. From a technology perspective the following four drivers are at work.

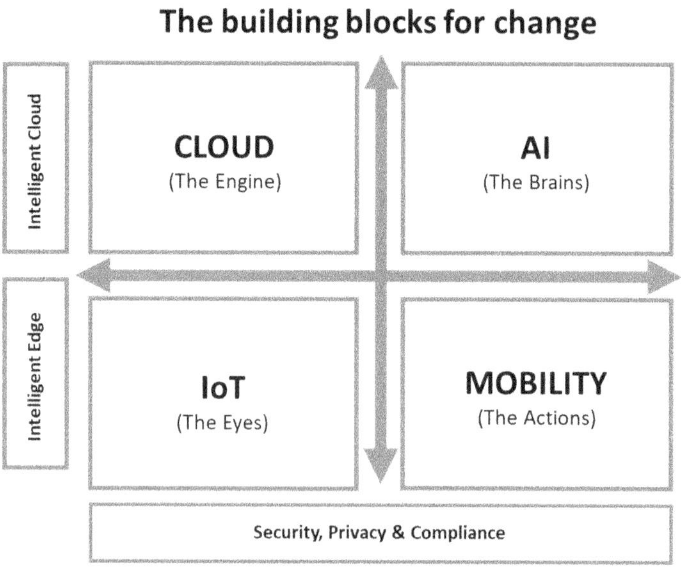

The building blocks for change

Intelligent Cloud	**CLOUD** (The Engine)	**AI** (The Brains)
Intelligent Edge	**IoT** (The Eyes)	**MOBILITY** (The Actions)
	Security, Privacy & Compliance	

Figure 4 - Building blocks for change

> One visible consequence of this is that we no longer need go to where the technology is (the office), rather the technology is all around us, it is part of us (the office is where we are).

---

[11] *https://go.forrester.com/age-of-the-customer/*
[12] (Zvika Krieger, n.d.) *https://www.weforum.org/centre-for-the-fourth-industrial-revolution/about*

Internet of Things (IoT)

The Internet of Things refers to the ever-growing network of physical objects that use internet connectivity, and the communication that occurs between these objects and other Internet-enabled devices and systems[13]. These "eyes on the world" allow information to be collected about everything, including us.

Cloud

Cloud refers to a model for enabling ubiquitous, convenient, on-demand network access to a shared pool of configurable computing resources (e.g., networks, servers, storage, applications, and services) that can be rapidly provisioned and released with minimal management effort or service provider interaction[14].

Artificial Intelligence, Analytics, Machine Learning

AI is the branch of computer science concerned with making computers behave like humans[15].

Analytics is the process of collecting, organising and analysing sets of data to discover patterns and other useful information.

ML is a type of artificial intelligence (AI) that provides systems with the ability to learn without being explicitly programmed. Enabling computers to find data, within data without human intervention[16].

Mobile

In 2016 Smartphones, tablets and IoT devices already accounted for more than 60 per cent of smart connected devices[17]. This has increased at a faster rate than expected, with predictions often failing to keep up with reality. However, "mobile" is not just about the devices, but also the ability to consume actions and outcomes, from any location. Whether that be humans using smart devices, robots in fields or remote valves turning off when a leak is detected.

---

[13] https://www.webopedia.com
[14] https://csrc.nist.gov/publications/detail/sp/800-145/final
[15] (https://www.webopedia.com
[16] https://www.webopedia.com
[17] https://technology.ihs.com/587841/more-than-six-billion-smartphones-by-2020-ihs-markit-says

Business Drivers

The business drivers may be anything from commercial dollars and cents to outcomes that have societal benefits. Whatever the drivers, to be embraced by stakeholders, they must be clear and concise and not wrapped in a shroud of deceit. If they are, your stakeholders will see right through it and you will lose their trust.

> Be clear about the reasons for change and the business drivers. Articulate these to all stakeholders and then act, as procrastination will leave you behind.

The following are examples of the drivers impacting businesses today:

- Business Transformation
  - Fundamentally rethinking what we do to improve how we do it?
  - Looking to transform rather than optimize
  - Using AI and BI to fundamentally analyse the Business (the Top BI Trends 2019[18] survey highlights where BI is being used)
- Digital Transformation[19]
  - Digital transformation used as a means for business transformation[20]
  - Unlocking digital silos to improve whole of business insights
  - Introduction of digital workers (Bots) into the business
  - Intelligent work processes to augment people with technology
  - Millennial effect of "Digital First"
  - A state of constant change leading to an Innovate or Die strategic approach

---

[18] *https://bi-survey.com/top-business-intelligence-trends*
[19] *http://www.industryweek.com/technology-and-iiot/unmasking-digital-transformation-6-b2b-drivers-2018*
[20] *https://www.cio.com/article/3198121/it-industry/whats-now-in-digital-transformation.html*

- Data Management & Governance[21]
  - o Data is considered a strategic asset. However, there is a growing expectation about the management of this data especially from a security and privacy. The poor management and protection of personal data has led to legislation being implemented in many countries and regions around the world
    e.g. GDPR (*https://gdpr-info.eu/*)
- Customer Experience (CX)
  - o Organisations such as Uber, Amazon and Netflix have changed the consumer expectation of how they interact with technology. As Brendan Witcher, Principal Analyst at Forrester explained, "Each time a consumer is exposed to an improved digital experience, their expectations are immediately reset to a new higher level." [22]
- Cyber Security
  - o While the cloud and mobile devices are essential components of any company's digital transformation, they do present a significant cybersecurity risk. "The direct costs commonly associated with data breaches are far less significant than the "hidden" costs. Research by Deloitte's suggests these account for less than 5 percent of the total business impact." [23]
- Regulatory environment[24]
  - o Regulatory challenges, ranging from privacy and security to taxation and data sovereignty, are no longer applicable to only highly regulated businesses. These sorts of regulation are now applicable to all businesses and, the power of the regulators is undeniable—their impact can be catalytic or catastrophic for businesses.

---

[21] *https://bi-survey.com/top-business-intelligence-trends*
[22] *https://www.cio.com/article/3198121/it-industry/whats-now-in-digital-transformation.html*
[23] *https://www2.deloitte.com/au/en/pages/media-releases/articles/business-impacts-cyber-attacks.html*
[24] *https://www2.deloitte.com/us/en/pages/technology-media-and-telecommunications/articles/technology-industry-outlook.html*

- Artificial Intelligence
  - "If you don't have an AI strategy, you're going to die in the world that's coming." eBay CEO Devin Wenig. "AI" - beyond the sci-fi connotations - is unclear to many.[25]
- Business Accountability and Transparency[26]
  - A renewed focus on business ethics, accountability, and transparency. Driven in part by an empowered consumer culture which is able, through the power of social media, to very quickly and decisively strike against any organisation caught, or perceived to be, acting inappropriately. The stakeholders are far more than just the shareholders.
- Robotic process automation enhances the human worker
  - RPA can create more time for resource-strapped workers. Repetitive and basic tasks in a traditional setting can take tens of thousands of hours to complete, software-enabled bots can accomplish these same tasks with rapid speed and infallible accuracy – saving time and costs. [27]

Shaping the new opportunities

Directors and senior executives have a pivotal role in shaping the conversation about how a business reacts to these opportunities.

Thinking forward the board need to make a strategic determination of where the business is today and the gap to where they want it to be in a world of disruptive influences, rather than a steady state one.

Understanding the current level of Entrepreneurial Intensity within the business, will help in assessing the ability to reach these future aspirations. The desired outcomes will determine whether innovation is focused on producing another iteration of the current product or fundamentally disrupting the industry?

---

[25] *https://www.cio.com/article/3198121/it-industry/whats-now-in-digital-transformation.html*

[26] *https://millmentor.com/33003-2/*

[27] *https://www.govloop.com/robotic-process-automation-enhancing-the-human-worker/*

The board also needs to be clear about whether their risk appetite is aligned to the level of changes that will be required?

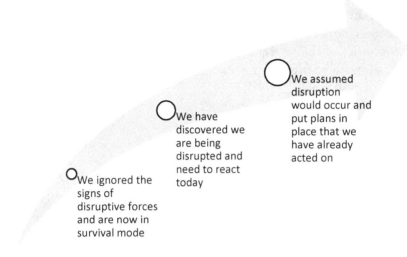

Figure 5 - Awareness of disruptive forces

Is it real? – Todays Opportunities

Finding the idea that will enable you to transform your business or industry may not be simple, however, if you don't do it someone else will.

> The future is already here - it's just not evenly distributed
>
> **William Gibson, 2003**

Here are examples of where change is happening today.

Aerospace

Airbus has been using technology in the aircraft they build for the last 20 years or more. Where the transformation came was in the optimisation of their factories and the design and manufacturing processes. They went further with this to understand the end user (Passenger) experience through collecting data from various social media and other sources. The data allowed them to make improvements which provided value to the airlines who purchase their aircraft. [28]

---

[28] *https://mashable.com/2016/03/24/airbus-airspace-cabin-design/#_PCy2W9DOsqT*

Mining

Rio Tinto[29] and BHP are using technology to create their "Digital Mines" [30] using autonomous trucks, trains, and drones to extract higher value from existing assets. Drones carry out land and infrastructure surveys, reducing the exposure of humans to risk. The internet of things enables real-time data capture with low-cost sensors that feed information back to core systems for analysis and action or response.

Agriculture

The industry is working[31] not only to optimise the water and soil conditions, but also pesticide management. Technologies such as IoT and AI can collect and analyse data, providing pest infestation predictions and pesticide recommendations to optimise yields. Specialist companies such as eVineyard[32], are providing industry specific solutions and countries such as Australia are leading[33] these global initiatives at a national level.

Health and Safety

ConnectiX[34] provide systems that track how, when and by who assets are managed across a supply chain. Data analysis can identify trends in incidents, leading to the implementation of preventative measures that can reduce the number of injuries and fatalities

Finance and Banking

Fintech[35] is transforming all areas of the finance and banking industry. Neobanks such as 86400 and Judo, discovery and execution platforms such as Likwidity, and "buy now, pay later" companies such as Afterpay are all fundamentally challenging the established players in the market. Whether these examples survive individually, only time will tell, however they are forcing the pace of transformation.

---

[29] https://www.riotinto.com/ourcommitment/smarter-technology-24275.aspx
[30] https://www.accenture.com/au-en/insight-resources-digital-transformation-future-mining
[31] https://blog.csiro.au/digital-agriculture-whats-all-the-fuss-about/
[32] https://www.evineyardapp.com/
[33] www.austrade.gov.au/ArticleDocuments/1358/Agriculture40-brochure.pdf
[34] https://www.connectix.com.au/service/
[35] https://en.wikipedia.org/wiki/Financial_technology

Imagine a world where...

The following table shares a few more examples. However, if you are still not convinced, then please spend some time in your favourite search engine, or shortcut the process and look at the blog post "Digital Transformation and Cloud Research – Summary of useful resources" [36] where Stephen Parker has collated hundreds of links to digital transformation resources and research.

You are directed to an available parking space that is reserved for you (significantly reducing congestion)

Smart Cities: Solving Urban Problems Using Technology (Palo Alto)

https://www.youtube.com/watch?v=nnyRZotnPSU

Insurance companies pay you GBP5,000 to put sensors in your home

Clause 14. Preventative Measures: We will pay: ...Up to GBP5,000 … towards the cost of alterations or installations… to prevent or mitigate future loss …

(UK Insurance company)

Robotic Dairy Farm Tours - Manawatu

"Cows are milked voluntarily, when they want to, up to 3 times a day, day and night by 3 Lely Astronaut A4 robots, after which the cows stroll back to the pasture"

https://www.newzealand.com/in/plan/business/robotic-dairy-farm-tours-manawatu/

2 tons of grapes are sorted in 12 minutes (vs two tons in an hour, using 15 human sorters)

"Then the future happened: a ten-foot-long, Willy Wonka-esque contraption called an optical grape sorter." (Jan 2014, Napa Valley)

https://modernfarmer.com/2014/01/robot-can-find-2-tons-perfect-grapes-12-minutes/

Figure 6 - Digital transformation in action

[36] *https://1visionot.com/2017/01/06/digital-transformation-and-cloud-research-summary-of-useful-resources/*

Chapter

Ideas are cheap

Great ideas alter the power balance in relationships. That's why great ideas are initially resisted

Hugh MacLeod (Co-Founder, GapingVoid)

Execution is the challenging part

L OOKING back in time, there are many examples of great people whose ideas were initially dismissed or considered outrageous but were subsequently accepted as the standard.

- 1543 - Nicolaus Copernicus – challenged the view that earth (and humanity) were positioned at the centre of the universe
- 1687 - Isaac Newton (and Gottfried Wilhelm Leibniz) provided the science that moved us from Aristotelian mechanics to what we now call classic mechanics
- 1859 – Charles Darwin's ideas moved us from goal-directed change to evolution by natural selection
- 1908 - Henry Ford introduced the assembly line which produced the Model T that converted the automobile from an expensive curiosity into a practical conveyance
- 1919 – Albert Einstein published theories that shifted the worldview from Newtonian gravity to General Relativity
- 1980 Bill Gates set the goal of "a computer on every desk and in every home" - what seemed like a wild leap at the time

Each of these challenged the status quo and in doing so created true paradigm shifts (Thomas Kuhn[37]). Once the initial objections were overcome, they become the basis for a new "normal" and provided the platform for waves of subsequent innovation and entrepreneurship.

Of course, it is not always easy to overcome the objections, it requires effort and often significant personal sacrifice. And whilst one of the characteristics of entrepreneurs is "vision", timing can also play a factor with great ideas sometimes failing to initially gain traction only to be established at a later date.

- The Apple Newton was launched in 1993 as a handheld personal digital assistant. It struggled both technically and commercially and was cancelled by Steve Jobs on his return to the beleaguered Apple in 1997. Ten years later the iPhone was launched delivering handheld computing to the masses and the rise of Apple to one of the world's most valuable companies.

Board Skills and Focus

A key part of a director's responsibilities is to ensure the business identifies when to wait and when to engage with new ideas and hence evolve to meet changing market needs and ensure the longevity of the organisation. The Bob Tricker model of Corporate Governance[38] outlines four key focus areas, one of which is Strategy Formulation (See top right, The Tricker Model).

However, it is all too easy for boards to become focused on internal and compliance activities (see bottom left, The Tricker Model). The risk is that this lack of outward focus can result in businesses missing the market changes, which allow new entrants or product substitutes to enter the market and challenge, or sometimes disrupt, the existing providers. Amazon exemplifies this constant innovation attitude with their "It's always day 1" philosophy[39]. This culture flows from the board, to the executive and through the organisation where new ideas are continually embraced and tested.

---

[37] *https://en.wikipedia.org/wiki/The_Structure_of_Scientific_Revolutions*
[38] *http://www.bobtricker.co.uk/corporate-governance.html*
[39] *https://www.forbes.com/sites/quora/2017/04/21/what-is-jeff-bezos-day-1-philosophy/*

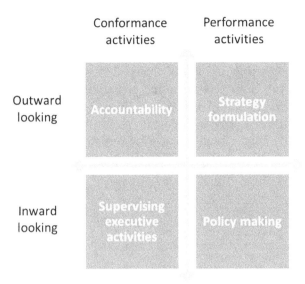

Bob Tricker, Corporate Governance

Figure 7 - The Tricker Model

A report[40] from the Australian Institute of Company Directors outlines five key recommendations for boards to improve their performance on innovation:

1. Lift directors' technology and digital literacy.
2. Set clear expectations of management regarding calculated risk-taking to drive innovation.
3. Develop a shared language with management, and clear narrative for investors/members on innovation.
4. Ensure innovation features regularly on boardroom agendas.
5. Establish a budget and executive incentives for long-term innovation.

> The longevity of any business today is under constant pressure from the ever-increasing rate of change. As a director, it is your responsibility to make sure your organization does not just survive but innovates and evolves.

---

[40] *https://aicd.companydirectors.com.au/membership/membership-update/a-wake-up-call-on-innovation*

Perception Filters

Change requires us to identify problems that are worth solving, but also ones that are solvable. However, we tend to see the world through the biases of our current models and understanding. This can create filters that prevent us from seeing the value and worth of new business ideas or from recognising technologies that enable new solutions. This results in business leaders being anchored to their current models and strategies and perceiving new approaches as being pointless endeavours and/or not viable.

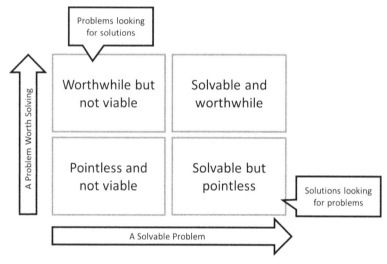

Figure 8 - Is the problem worth solving and is it solvable?

As an example, if in 2001[41] you had asked the owner of a HiFi[42] shop if there was a market for a device with small speakers, a tiny amplifier and a lossy sound compression system you would have been laughed at. Their experience (perception filter) would say customers walk into their shop aspiring to the top end systems and then compromise based on their budget. Yet today we live in a world of smart devices, streaming music and the HiFi shop being a rare sight on our high streets.

> "If I had asked people what they wanted, they would have said faster horses."
>
> **Henry Ford (maybe!)**

---

[41] The first Apple iPod was released in October 2001)
[42] *https://en.wikipedia.org/wiki/High_fidelity* (for those wondering!!)

Breaking away from your perception filters

Once established, our cognitive biases[43] often operate at a sub-conscious level. Therefore, we need to develop conscious and formal approaches to both recognize and challenge them, whether as individuals or as a team.

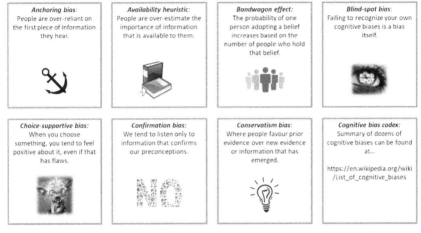

Figure 9 - Cognitive biases

There are two areas of focus when removing the filters. Firstly, reframing the problem to make sure there is clarity on what the problem is, and the impact it presents. The second is the validity of the problem, and weather it is a problem or a symptom, and is it worth solving.

"Perception filters supress objectivity and restrict entrepreneurial thinking."

David Cleminson

How much control do we really have?

In established markets there is a natural tension between competitors within the market and their relationships with suppliers and buyers. Brand reputation with buyers, bargaining power with suppliers, quality and efficiency of processes all play a part in establishing a hierarchy within the market. Businesses focus on incremental improvements, so they can gain market share from their rivals. However, it is the very process improvements that

---

[43] *https://en.wikipedia.org/wiki/List_of_cognitive_biases*

create leaders that can in turn create inertia. Paradoxically, it can be the very best in a market, anchored to their "world leading processes" that can be most at risk of disruption from new entrants or substitute offerings.

Porters Five Forces Model

This tension is summarized in the Porters Five Forces model[44].

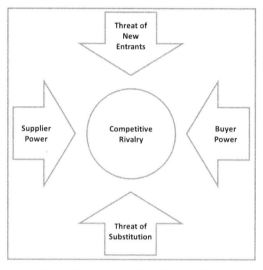

Figure 10 - Porter's Five Forces Model

The ever-increasing capability and adoption of technology has created opportunities for increased innovation. This has led to a rise in threats from new entrants, substitute offerings and a change in the bargaining power of buyers and suppliers.

- Buyers have been empowered through the availability of information and services on a global scale. This has led to what Forrester refer to as the "Age of the Customer"[45]
- Traditional barriers to entry such as access to capital to purchase hardware and software have been removed with the availability of Anything as a Service.
- Competitive advantages such as hard-earned discounts with traditional suppliers can be negated when start-up competitors use new "pay as you need" suppliers such as Amazon or Azure.

---

[44] *https://en.wikipedia.org/wiki/Porter%27s_five_forces_analysis*
[45] *https://go.forrester.com/age-of-the-customer/*

- Automation through the internet of things, robotics and artificial intelligence can fundamentally change the competitive advantage of resource intensive businesses.
- Effective use of social media channels can alter the value of traditional market influencer relationships
- Online marketplaces such as Google Play and Apple App Store have provided global reach to even the smallest of businesses.
- Companies like Amazon, eBay and Alibaba are providing global distribution and logistics capability to businesses of any size.
- Services such as WeWork allow businesses of any size to have "offices" around the world.

The "steady state" where tensions are understood and in balance, is being replaced by:

- Transformation, where new strains are appearing, being recognized and then proactively acted upon
- Disruption, where you don't know what you don't know until it is potentially too late, requiring reactive actions

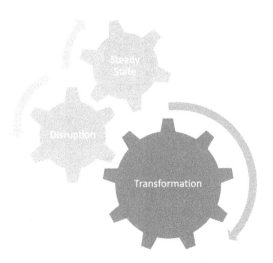

Figure 11 - Transformation and disruption

Will a robot take your job?

We can see how this might play out from research that considers the possibility of roles being replaced by robotics and automation. An example shared by the BBC in September 2015[46] considers the likelihood of a role being replaced by automation in the next five years. It is interesting that a number of the most at-risk roles are in the legal and financial professions which have traditionally been considered desirable and well remunerated.

Rank	Role	Automation Risk
1	Telephone salesperson	99%
2	Typist or related keyboard worker	99%
3	Legal secretary	98%
4	Financial accounts manager	98%
5	Weigher, grader or sorter	98%
6	Routine inspector and tester	98%
7	Sales administrator	97%
8	Book-keeper, payroll manager or wages clerk	97%
9	Finance officer	97%
10	Pensions and insurance clerk	97%

Figure 12 - Jobs at risk to automation

These changes are pulling the Porters Five Forces model out of shape and creating an advantage for new entrants and businesses with substitute offerings.

Does your Business Strategy and Model need to change?

The changes in market forces mean that just because your current strategy and business model is best of breed against the established market, does not mean it is fit for purpose going forward. This phenomenon is not new, businesses do not last "forever", and the timeframe for remaining relevant is getting shorter.

---

[46] https://www.bbc.com/news/technology-34066941

How Disruption happens

When disruption happens, you need to be listening for the signals amidst the noise. It may not be loud or explicit, but it will be there. McKinsey[47] have mapped the stages of disruption for an incumbent and the journey this will take them on. Where are you in the process? Have you planned for this?

Disruption introduces an incumbent to a new journey.

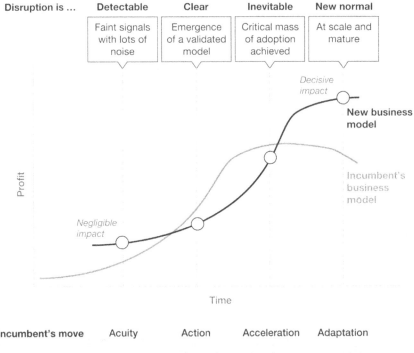

Figure 13 - Stages of Disruption

[47] *https://www.mckinsey.com/business-functions/strategy-and-corporate-finance/our-insights/an-incumbents-guide-to-digital-disruption*

Is your industry at risk?

The Harvard Business Review[48] published an article that considered how likely an industry is to be disrupted. Which quadrant is your industry in? Are you durable, viable, vulnerable or volatile?

Unless you have done the research, how can you be confident that your business is OK. When was the last time you surveyed your customers and truly looked at the answers and not just the filtered results that are presented in the Board Report? This lack of detailed interrogation has been a criticism in recent reviews such as the 2019 Royal Commission into banking in Australia. These are summarised in the Australian Institute of Directors: Essential Director Update – 18[49].

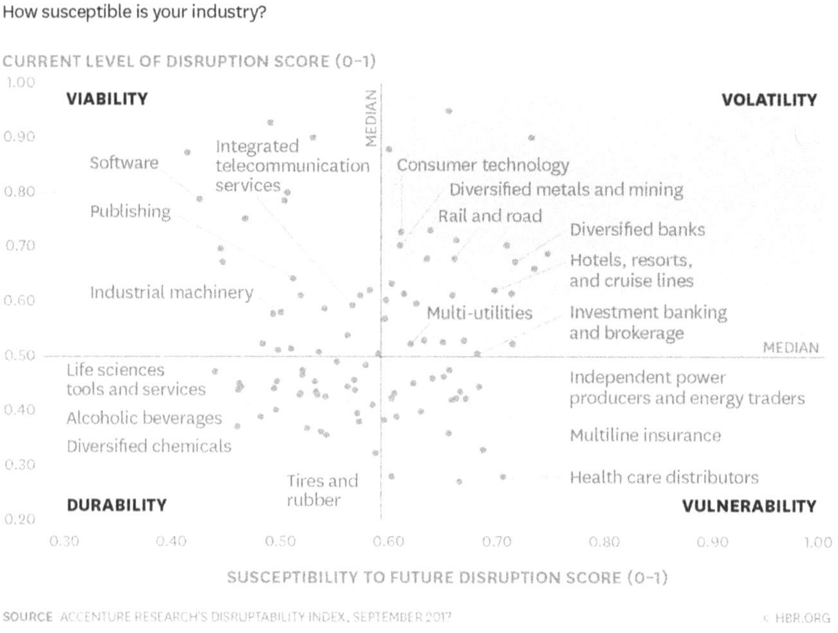

How susceptible is your industry?

CURRENT LEVEL OF DISRUPTION SCORE (0-1)

Figure 14 - The Four Stages of Disruption

The decisions you make now could be the difference between transformation and disruption.

---

[48] *https://hbr.org/2018/01/how-likely-is-your-industry-to-be-disrupted-this-2x2-matrix-will-tell-you*

[49] *https://aicd.companydirectors.com.au/-/media/cd2/resources/events/essential-director-update/pdf/essential-director-update-presentation-2018.ashx*

How relevant are you today?

The relevance of a business to its customers changes over time. Michael McQueen[50] has called this the Relevancy Curve.

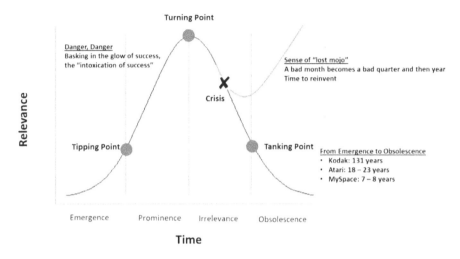

Figure 15 - Tipping, turning or tanking?

- At the **Tipping point** your offerings and brand gain traction in the market
- Growth leads to the moment when you can "bask in the glow of success"
- However, this is the time of danger, when others seeing your success become more competitive
- Without realizing it the **Turning point** can be passed. Poor results are dismissed as anomalous.
- This is the time for reinvention, before the slide towards the Tanking **point** becomes irreversible.

Long lived businesses have been through this cycle multiple times both at the macro level and for specific products.

---

[50] *https://www.youtube.com/watch?v=-zR7reXnQsY*

Blackberry – a tanking story

The fall of Blackberry from pre-eminence to forgotten player demonstrates this well. When Barack Obama became president in 2009 the news was full of stories about how he would be using a Blackberry[51]. It would be reasonable to say that Blackberry were "basking in the glow of success". However, they had not planned for or reacted well to the arrival of competitors such as the iPhone. Within 4 years their once dominant market share[52] and high-flying share price[53] had "tanked". Whilst the business has "survived" their share price has not recovered (from over USD 70 in 2009 to USD7.35 as at December 2018) and their market share is still essentially zero[54].

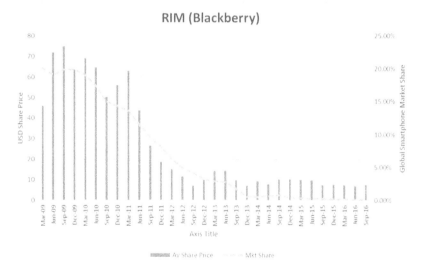

Figure 16 - Blackberry's Tanking Story

[51] https://www.theguardian.com/world/2009/jan/21/barack-obama-blackberry-national-security

[52] https://www.statista.com/statistics/263439/global-market-share-held-by-rim-smartphones/

[53] https://www.macrotrends.net/stocks/charts/BB/blackberry/stock-price-history

[54] https://www.businessinsider.com.au/blackberry-smartphone-marketshare-zero-percent-gartner-q4-2016-2017-2

Microsoft – a reinvention story

Microsoft offer the alternative "reinvention" story. In the late 1990s Microsoft had established a near monopoly with Windows and Office. Despite this position and with huge revenue and profit, their share price languished for over ten years. It took the threat of substitute offerings in the form of "cloud solutions" and new entrants such as Amazon, before Microsoft was forced to react. The process was a challenging one and required significant changes to culture, strategy and senior management. A pivotal change was the replacement of Steve Ballmer with Satya Nadella as the CEO. For shareholders, this reinvention has been a very positive outcome with the share price moving from $30 in early 2013 to over $100 at the end of 2018.

Figure 9 - Microsoft's Reinvention

Figure 17 - Microsoft's Reinvention

Average time for a company in the S&P 500[55]

Change has been ever present in all industries, however, there has been a significant increase in the rate of change since the mid 20th century. One visualization of this has been the average age of a company on the S&P 500. According to analysts at Credit Suisse[56] "The average age of a company listed on the S&P 500 has fallen from almost 60 years in the 1950s to less than 20 years currently"

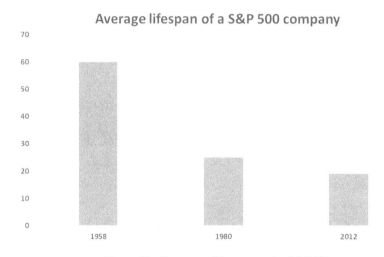

Figure 18 - Company lifespan on the S&P 500

> You used to have decades to spot the crisis between Turning and Tanking; now you only have years or even months. The outcome is that there needs to be a constant focus on "what you don't know, you don't know."

[55] *https://infogram.com/average-life-span-of-sandp-500-companies-1g143mn455742zy*
[56] *https://research-doc.credit-suisse.com/docView?language=ENG&format=PDF&sourceid=csplusresearchcp&documen t_id=1079753961&serialid=0FaMPipwKOHKsuTLB1cQRu0GKKYVKgdRcvdIgMP RbEs%3D*

To build or consume

For many areas of business, the outsourced or external supplier is the default choice.

- While the physical product may be core to a company, the delivery logistics rarely are. So, this process is outsourced to companies such as FedEx.
- The history of banking dates back to around 2000 BC[57], and since then (with a few exceptions) it has been considered less risky to store your assets in a secure facility rather than "under a mattress" or a small safe in a wall.
- Share certificates are now stored electronically by stock exchanges, equating to trillions of dollars of assets and people's personal wealth.

However, Information Technology & Communications (IT&C) services have until recently been delivered mainly "in-house". Even when standard software was used, it was still installed on servers within the business premises. This creates CAPEX constraints, even for the largest of businesses.

Now with most IT&C services available "as a service", outsourcing your technology is not prohibitive. You can choose what services you want to maintain internally and what you want to outsource. With many, traditionally core services, such as ERP and CRM now available via a Software as a Service (SaaS) model, you do not need to worry about the hardware, software, patching, databases, etc; as this is all managed and maintained for you.

XaaS[58] is not a one size and type fits all.

However, moving all your systems to the cloud or other emerging technologies is not necessarily the answer. You need a strategy based on the architecture and investments in your current system. You also need to consider the security and compliance commitments to your stakeholders.

- Will standardized "as a Service" offerings provide a competitive advantage through speed to market?

---

[57] *https://en.wikipedia.org/wiki/History_of_banking*
[58] *https://simple.wikipedia.org/wiki/Everything_as_a_service*

- Is there unique IP and business value in developing a custom solution?
- If you deliver solutions in-house do you already have the resources and skills within your business, or will you need to train existing and/or recruit new?

Each of these have compromises and pay-offs and it is likely that some sort of hybrid approach will be the optimal solution.

One way of envisaging this is to consider our own personal transport options.

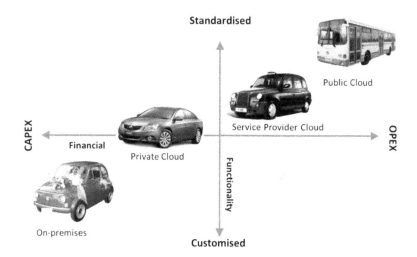

Figure 19 - Technology strategy model options

Public Transport (Public Cloud Services): A bus moves people from A to B via a set route and cannot alter or customise the course. It has specific attributes you can use; however, the service is standard, and you pay for the services based on how much you use it, without worrying about underlaying operating costs.

Taxi (Service Provider Cloud): A Taxi is more flexible in that it will pick you up and drop you anywhere within its operational areas. However, you still have no choice on specifics such as the model of vehicle, the driver etc). The costs are typically higher than using the "shared service" bus, but again you only pay for what you use, with no concerns for underlaying costs.

Leased/Company Car (Private Cloud): There are some limitations on models available, but you have the use of the entire car. You can use it to drive wherever you want to go and are not restricted to its use (subject to company or leasing policies). You are responsible for the day to day operational costs of the car, although underlaying maintenance is typically covered by a fixed price service plan. You are typically locked into a multi-year, fixed cost, paid on a monthly basis, with fees associated with backing out early.

Personal Car (On-Premises): You have a choice of everything in the market, and you can customise it the way you want it to look and perform. You can use it to drive whenever and wherever you want. However, you are responsible for all operational costs associated with the car. Your real choices are also limited by your budget, which is determined by your capacity to clear the capital costs, either directly or via a loan.

A bit of everything (Hybrid): Of course, in the real world we tend to use a combination of all of these. It may be convenient to drive to the train station, but we then take the train to the CBD or airport. If we are going out to a party, we may choose to take a taxi. A hybrid system is made up of a combination of the (architectures) characteristics of the vehicles as a method of managing your costs.

Planning your journey

Your organisation needs to have a transformation strategy in place before you start your journey. This would include initially understanding your existing system's issues, all the legal and Industry compliance, data protection and privacy obligations relating to both your business and your customer's organisations. Asking the right questions at the outset will determine the success of your transformation journey. Remember, change is hard for most people, with an organisation it is even more difficult, however, with an appropriate process, it is achievable.

> It's not simple to migrate your systems to the cloud and other emerging technologies. If you don't plan and understand problems before you start, they will be exacerbated and remain with you.

Change is a process

Change does not just happen. It needs leadership, vision, and process. It needs to include all stakeholders, internal and external. Where are you in the process?

At a board level, there are several decisions to be made, among them are determining if the organisation is ready to change, the board's appetite for risk, how progress will be monitored and critically who will take ownership of the transformation.

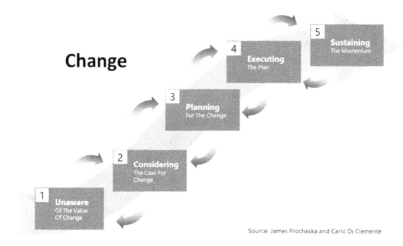

Source: James Prochaska and Carlo Di Clemente

Figure 20 - Change is not easy

You need to consider the skills within your organization at all levels from the Board to the shop floor. Your supplier relationships will need to be reviewed and possibly changed. Can your existing partners support your transformation, or will they be a constraint? These questions are critical to the success of the project.

Although some new entrants to the market could be considered a threat, others could be partners for procuring or delivering new services. A SWOT analysis could identify which new entrants could be new suppliers or customers, and which are threats.

Maintaining motivation during the change process, across both internal and external stakeholders, will be a critical factor for both short and long term success.

Creative Thinking

If I had an hour to solve a problem, I'd spend 55 minutes thinking about the problem and 5 minutes thinking about solutions."

Albert Einstein, Theoretical Physicist. 1879 – 1955

Although most businesses describe staff as their most valuable asset, for the most part they are not encouraged to think creatively about changing the way they do their job. After all, if everyone started deciding they had a better way to do things, chaos would soon follow. We share the well-established process and expect them to follow the rules.

Even when we ask them to "Be creative and think outside the square", it can be too limiting as there is often an unspoken constraint that implies the solution is still near the current model. Many reward systems are designed to incentivise zero defect, no error outcomes and to punish failure. This lack of incentive to find the breaking points or risk failure is a key blocker in the innovation process[59].

Whether we are acting as entrepreneurs or intrapreneurs, identifying transformational opportunities requires conscious creative thinking. We need to encourage people to ask "why do we do it like this", "what if it wasn't impossible". However, this can be disruptive to existing business cultures.

How many pieces of cake can you get with just 4 cuts?

Figure 21 - Thinking laterally

---

[59] *https://hbr.org/2002/08/the-failure-tolerant-leader*

If you answered 8 then congratulations, you have provided the "back of the book" answer. If you are a little more creative, then you can get to 12, 14 or 16. However, what rules or conditions have you imposed on yourself that are NOT included in the question, that if removed could result in millions of pieces?

- Do the instructions say equal size pieces?
- Do the instructions say straight cuts?

What if you had a nanometre wide piece of wire and made repeated circular or up-and-down cuts in multiple directions?

It is these common cognitive biases that can be significant blockers to change, both at the individual and organisational level. However, it's no good blaming this after the fact. You need to act now.

Being creative, is focusing on the questions, not the answers:

> It is essential to remind yourself, that as directors and organisational leaders, you have a responsibility to shape the future direction of your business, as well as ensuring it's success today

Chapter

Ask the Smart Questions

If I have seen further it is by standing on the shoulders of giants

Isaac Newton (Scientist, 1643 – 1727)

S MART Questions is about giving you valuable insights or "the Smarts". Usually these are only gained through years of painful and costly experience. Whether you already have a general understanding of the subject and need to take it to the next level or are starting from scratch, you need to make sure you ask the Smart Questions. We aim to short-circuit that learning process, by providing the expertise of the 'giants' that Isaac Newton referred to.

Not all the questions will necessarily be new or staggeringly insightful. The value you get from the information will undoubtedly vary. It depends on your job role and previous experience. We call this the 3Rs.

The 3 Rs

Some of the questions will be in areas where you know the answers already, so the book will **Reinforce** them in your mind.

You may have forgotten some aspects of the subject, so the book will **Remind** you.

Other questions may **Reveal** new insights to you that you've never considered before.

How do you use Smart Questions?

The structure of the questions is set out in Chapter 4, and the questions are in Chapters 5 to 7. The questions are laid out in a series of structured and ordered tables with the questions in one column and the explanation of why it matters alongside. We've also provided a checkbox so that you can mark which questions are relevant to your situation.

A quick scan down the column of questions should give you a general feel of where you are for each question vs. the 3Rs.

At the highest level they are a sanity check or checklist of areas to consider. You can take them with you to board meetings or use as the basis for reviews of specific projects. Just one question may save you a whole heap of cash or heartache.

We trust that you will find real insights. There may be some "aha" moments. Hopefully not too many sickening, head in the hands "what have we done' moments. Even if you do find yourself in such a situation, the questions may help you to re-establish some order, take control and steer yourself back into calmer waters.

In this context, probably the most critical role of the Smart Questions is to reveal risks that you might not have considered. On the flip side they should also open your thinking to opportunities that hadn't yet occurred to you. Balancing the opportunities and the risks, and then agreeing what is realistically achievable is the key to formulating an effective strategy.

The questions could be used in your internal meetings to inform or at least prompt the debate. Alternatively, they could shape the discussion you have with your suppliers, stakeholders or business partners.

How to dig deeper

Need more information? Not convinced by the examples, or want ones that are more relevant to your specific situation? Why not contact the Authors? They are, after all, the domain experts whose knowledge has raised your interest. For more details contact Smart Questions at *info@smart-questions.com* or the authors directly at *dcleminson@stratosquo.com.au* and *stephen@smart-questions.com.*

And finally

Please remember that these questions are **NOT** intended to be a prescriptive list that must be followed slavishly from beginning to end. It is also inevitable that the list of questions is not exhaustive, and we are confident that with the help of the community the list of Smart Questions will grow.

If you want to rephrase a question to improve its context or have identified a question we have missed, then let us know so we can add it to the collective knowledge.

We also understand that not all the questions will apply to all readers and all businesses. However, we encourage you to read them all as there may be a nugget of truth that can be adapted to your circumstances.

Above all we do hope that it provides a guide or a pointer to the areas that may be valuable to you and helps with the "3 Rs".

Chapter

Introduction to the Questions

Any time, any place, anywhere

Martini drinks advert (1970 – 1980s)

THE set of questions that follow are separated into 3 broad sections. The first set are designed to help you think about the direct implications of digital transformation for your organization. The second set relate to the broader, external marketplace of your customers and stakeholders. The third set provide a more detailed technology context, but they are NOT intended to be "techie", rather they are intended to help shape the technology conversation.

Chapter 5: Questions for my organisation

1. Motivation
2. Reframing the Problem
3. Board oversight
4. Business model and strategy

Chapter 6: Marketplace questions

1. Supply chain
2. Accountability and Legal
3. Digital Transformation Technology Partners

Chapter 7: Digital Landscape Questions

1. Asking the Big High-level questions.
2. The Technical questions not to be scared to ask?
3. Cyber Security, Security & Privacy

Chapter

Questions for my organisation

Any fool can know. The point is to understand

Albert Einstein (Theoretical physicist, 1879 - 1955)

WITH digital transformation not just on the horizon, but happening now, there are questions which should be asked to provide clarity and insight about the changes that will occur within the business. The requirement for scrutiny and oversight within a business should be ever present. However, it is easy to "take your eye of the ball" and fall into a business as usual mindset, where bad habits can creep in as businesses try to enhance their share of the current market. Recent examples in the banking sector highlight this lack of scrutiny:

- Wells Fargo, where 3.5m fake accounts were created to help reach cross-selling sales targets, resulting in initial (and potentially growing) fines of USD185m[60]
- The Australian banking sector that has been subject to a Royal Commission. The final report[61] has been very critical of the failings in holding banking entities to account

During periods of change, successful businesses demonstrate the ability to adapt. However, this enhanced level of agility, if unmanaged, can also lead to potentially damaging levels of risk. This should NOT be an excuse to fail to act, but it does increase the requirement for scrutiny and oversight.

---

[60] *https://en.wikipedia.org/wiki/Wells_Fargo_account_fraud_scandal*
[61] *https://financialservices.royalcommission.gov.au/Pages/reports.aspx*

5.1 Motivation

Before embarking on the journey of change, have you considered the compelling reasons for the change? In section 5.2 we discuss reframing the problem. This is part of analysing the reasons and motivation for change, resulting in clarity and

Figure 22 - Motivation

understanding which will add to the refinement of the narrative. With effective leadership, clear direction, consideration of possible implications and the appropriate motivation, change to the business has a higher opportunity for success.

"If you don't know where you're going, any road'll take you there"

(Chapter 6 of Lewis Carroll's Alice's Adventures in Wonderland)

Unless you have clearly articulated your motivation, then it will be challenging to bring all your stakeholders *(including your customers, exec's employees & investors.)* along for the ride with you.

☒	Question	Why this matters
☐	5.1.1 What is creating the motivation for change?	There are many reasons for change including: • Cultural • Social • Legal • Economic • Political • Technological • Disruption Whatever your motivations they need to be clearly communicated to avoid speculation and shadow communication, both internally and externally.
☐	5.1.2 What is the Board's appetite for risk?	The boards appetite for risk should be an upfront consideration, as part of the motivation for proceeding with a digital transformation. The board and in turn the C-suite will set the tone for change both internally and externally.
☐	5.1.3 Is there new government legislation forcing change in our business?	Changes to government requirements & legislation may force the change in approach or how the business operates. Proactively monitoring the legislative change process may provide months (or even years) notice. This will not only smooth the transformation process but potentially provide a competitive advantage.
☐	5.1.4 Are there overseas changes that create a requirement for us to change?	New legislation such as the implementation of GDPR[62] in Europe, can impose change even if indirectly. We may choose to adapt our market approach to take advantage of these requirements OR consider leaving a market if it is prohibitive to try and meet the requirements.

[62] https://gdpr-info.eu/

☒	Question	Why this matters
☐	5.1.5 Is there an economic change forcing us to pivot?	Changes to both the local and overseas economies can force businesses to pivot and look to more lucrative markets or change the product set to fit the economic landscape. The rise of the Asian and Chinese markets has already had a significant impact on global markets.
☐	5.1.6 What digital transformation activities are our competitors undertaking?	Without a detailed understanding of our competitors' activities we do not know whether we are thought leading or action lagging, too early or too late. Also be aware of the quiet ones, there silence may not be a sign of inaction, but rather stealth.
☐	5.1.7 What is the risk if our competitors solve the problem before us?	There may be advantages to be a first mover. Alternatively, there may be benefits of being a "fast follower", allowing others to make the mistakes. Whether you are leading or following you need to have intelligence on what your current competitors are doing AND keep looking for new entrants (Porters 5 Forces)
☐	5.1.8 Is this change to support a dwindling bottom line, or is it a long term strategy?	It is advantageous to be honest with yourselves when making tough decisions. Whether they are tactical or strategic long term changes, you can't fool, yourselves.
☐	5.1.9 Are there new entrants to our market with disruptive strategies?	While we are focused on our traditional competitors, new entrants can enter the market unseen. Online software has disrupted traditional businesses such as accounting (www.xero.com). Online shopping (www.amazon.com) has been disruptive to high street shops. On-demand services (www.netflix.com) have forced change on the media industry. Transformation becomes disruption when you don't see it coming.

☒	Question	Why this matters
☐	5.1.10 Are there companies with substitute/ replacement offerings?	Much like new entrants, substitute offerings can reduce the value of our existing strengths and market position. For example, we may have operated the most efficient photo printing shop. But when photo film was replaced by digital images and online sharing, people largely stopped printing pictures and our strengths became irrelevant.
☐	5.1.11 Are our customer expectations driving change in our business?	Our customers may be vocal, and we may be listening. However, this is not always the case and we may be blissfully ignorant and/or wilfully deaf. Using the appropriate feedback research from your customer base will help to quantify and justify the need for change. One of the risks is that your current customers may not want change today, but will complain if you have not transformed tomorrow.
☐	5.1.12 How would we like the market to perceive our approach to change?	This relates back to the appetite for risk, whether we want to control or dominate the industry, or, we want to let others go through the effort and pain of change, then follow. We may have built a conservative reputation with our customer base, is this what we want, or is this an opportunity to shift? If we are seen as a thought leader, how important is to be on the bleeding vs leading edge?
☐	5.1.13 Are our suppliers forcing us to change?	Is there pressure from your suppliers to change the way you operate or the business model you are currently using is not compatible with their new model.

☒	Question	Why this matters
☐	5.1.14 Is there a requirement to change the culture within our business?	Legacy businesses may need to undergo a transformation due to culture challenges (e.g. impact on customer service). This may result in a digital transformation to support the changing expectations of current customers or the opportunities from new ones. It may be the changing expectations of the next generation of employees. Global expansion may require different styles of communication to align with a distributed and diverse work force.

5.2 Reframing the Problem

Are we reacting to a symptom or the true underlaying cause? Before we start the Digital Transformation journey, we need to make sure we understand the core reasons and desired outcomes, so we can be sure we are addressing the right "Problem". [63]

There are many problem-solving methodologies and models, but for its simplicity we like the one from a presentation titled "Operating Advantage Problem Solving" [64] shared by Larry Thompson[65].

Figure 23 - 7 step approach to problem solving

---

[63] https://hbr.org/2012/09/are-you-solving-the-right-problem
[64] https://www.slideshare.net/LarryThompsonMfgT/ps-130-rev-d-problem-solving-61385967
[65] https://www.linkedin.com/in/lvthompson/

☒	Question	Why this matters
☐	5.2.1 Is this really a problem?	It is important not to ignore or procrastinate when a challenge occurs, however we also need to be careful that we don't "knee-jerk" react to a situation before we consider the real implications.
☐	5.2.2 Are we addressing the right problem?	Within organisations there are many problems which could be solved. The challenge is identifying which of them need to be solved?
☐	5.2.3 Are we clear about the objectives and desired outcomes and are they self-consistent?	Question the objective. If we are going to spend the time and effort solving problems, we need to have a clear objective to ensure we have a clear focus and measurable KPIs.
☐	5.2.4 Is the problem worth solving?	Just because a problem can be solved does not mean it is worth solving. Problems with a high frequency of occurrence and a high business impact when they occur, should be a higher priority than low occurrence, low impact ones.
☐	5.2.5 What is the business impact of doing nothing?	Will the time and effort of solving the problem, make a difference to the business and bring improvements or efficiencies. It's no use spending a $1,000,000 on a $1,000 problem.
☐	5.2.6 Is the problem solvable?	A problem may be worth solving, but it may not be solvable either in absolute terms (e.g. the laws of physics, as we know them, just don't allow it) or due to other constraints (e.g. technology capability).
☐	5.2.7 Have we established legitimacy?	Vision and ownership from "the top" are critical during any period of change. However, it is important to bring the wider business along as well. Making sure we get input from a diverse group of people within the organisation, will ensure we see the problems and priorities from multiple perspectives.

☒	Question	Why this matters
☐	5.2.8 Have we brought outsiders into the discussion?	The increasing power of external stakeholders means that it important to invite them to the conversation to give a wider perspective.
☐	5.2.9 Have we validated stakeholder understanding of the problem?	It is easy for effort to be wasted due the lack of a common description/ understanding of a problem. Articulating the definition of the problem in writing, will provide a shared understanding and allow for further dialog.
☐	5.2.10 Have we asked what's missing?	It is easy to overlook aspects of a problem. This can occur at the outset, but also as time progresses and the problem evolves. It is important that we keep checking we have a clear picture of the problem.
☐	5.2.11 Have we considered the context of this problem; has it been categorised properly?	In most cases the problem people discuss is part of, or a symptom of other deeper problems. Categorising problems helps to understand these relationships, which may in turn change the impact and scope of the problem.
☐	5.2.12 What resources do we need, to deliver a solution for the problem?	There are many ways and means to solving problems. The optimal solution may vary based on the ability to utilise existing resources or the need to add new ones. However, we need to be careful not to forego long term benefits by being anchored to the short-term benefits of retaining existing resources.
☐	5.2.13 Does addressing the problem create additional benefits and opportunities?	If our organisation is having a problem, there is a good chance other organisations are having a similar issue. The choice of solution to the core problem may contribute to solving other issues and open opportunities for competitive advantage.
☐	5.2.14 Can we turn this problem into an opportunity?	Analyse positive exceptions. Take the opportunity to think beyond the solution. Take the view that a problem is an opportunity to be taken advantage of.

5.3 Board oversight

Figure 24 - Board oversight

Oversight is a central responsibility of the board. In times of change the status quo is being tested and transformed and to ensure that "oversight" is fit for purpose there needs to be greater scrutiny, with an enhanced level of interrogation and questioning. The Royal Commission into banking in Australia[66] has been highly critical of boards that have failed to provide the effective oversight that is expected.

> As a board member you have a responsibility to the business to provide oversight to make sure the business meets its commitments as per its charter not only from a financial perspective, but from a non-financial and cultural perspective as well.

---

[66] *https://financialservices.royalcommission.gov.au/Pages/reports.aspx*

[X]	Question	Why this matters
☐	5.3.1 Is there a clear guiding light that will direct our oversight?	If digital transformation is impacting and/or changing our business strategy and models, then this may change the priorities and focus of oversight. For example, a shift of focus from internal efficiencies to customer satisfaction.
☐	5.3.2 Does the board have a defined posture related to technology risk?	Technology is now an integral part of business operations. Technology failures and risks can bring the business to its knees just as much as financial and legal issues.
☐	5.3.3 Does the board have a defined posture related to cyber-security risks?	Security incidents can among other things result in disruption to critical services and loss of data. This does not just have an operational and financial impact but can cause significant reputational and stakeholder damage. A detailed understanding is required at the highest levels to ensure breaches are not "pushed under the carpet".
☐	5.3.4 How far does technology oversight need to reach into the supply chain?	Businesses are no longer technology islands. Information is passed between multiple parties. A risk in one area of these interconnected relationships can have an impact elsewhere. It may be necessary to have oversight into these external services and/or define standards that must be met to ensure safety and reliability of the whole chain.
☐	5.3.5 What are the defined outcomes expected from the Digital strategy	To get the best possible outcomes, we need to have a clearly articulated digital strategy which is precisely aligned and developed as part of the business strategy. It must clearly articulate the specific outcomes as part of the business strategy.

☒	Question	Why this matters
☐	5.3.6 Is our governance model supportive of a more agile approach to the business?	With the change in business models and methods, have we looked at the evolution of our governance model to support our organisation in the future?
☐	5.3.7 Do we need to increase the focus on strategy within our governance model?	Supervisory and compliance activities are a critical part of the board's role. However, the ongoing success of the business also requires a focus on strategy. This is especially true during times of change when adjustments to strategy may be required as lessons are learnt.
☐	5.3.8 Does the frequency of board meetings need to change?	Our current meeting schedule may not provide the level of agility required as the business changes. A higher frequency may be during critical periods, with dynamic agendas.
☐	5.3.9 Does the board's meeting agenda need to be updated?	Business transformation is, by definition, not "business as usual", there may be new areas that need focus either as a temporary item during the change process or possibly ongoing.
☐	5.3.10 Do we need to review our sub-committees?	The scope and charter for existing sub-committees may need to be updated. Additional sub-committees may be required to provide the detailed review and feedback to the board.
☐	5.3.11 Have we carried out a skills audit and gap analysis for the current board?	It can be challenging; however, we may not have all the skills required within the current board membership. We may be strong in legal and financial, but what about technical, cyber-security, privacy. These have traditionally been specialist "external" skills, however the importance of technology to businesses means a strong understanding is key to ensure the correct oversight and to allow problem shaping to occur.

X	Question	Why this matters
☐	5.3.12 How do we ensure that the digital strategy remains aligned to the business strategy and how can it be measured along the way?	What will the framework be to make sure these strategies remain aligned to deliver business value and how will they be monitored along the way?
☐	5.3.13 Have we considered using an external organisation to upskill the board members on digital transformation and technology?	Having an understanding of the key concepts may be sufficient to allow the board to ask the probing questions of the operational teams that ensures accurate insights are gained.
☐	5.3.14 Do we need to challenge our cognitive biases[67]?	At all levels of the business it is easy for biases to be embedded that limit the ability to embrace change and see alternatives. At the board and senior executive level this can be especially impactful during a process of change and can prevent effective problem shaping and oversight. The introduction of a specialist leadership program may be helpful in exposing these biases and providing tools to address them.
☐	5.3.15 Have we considered a temporary advisory board?	An advisory board may allow the specialist skills of independent advisors to be part of the oversight process, without changing the current board structure. This could provide a pipeline for new board members and/or remain in place as a long-term strategy if there are limited places at the boardroom table.

---

[67] *https://en.wikipedia.org/wiki/List_of_cognitive_biases*

☒	Question	Why this matters
☐	5.3.16 Are we making effective use of technology to support our governance activities?	Tools such as a "Board Portal" may assist in the management and review of greater volumes of information, the requirement for easy access to past "paperwork" such as minutes and the organisation of meetings that may be more frequent or irregular and may not always be easy to arrange in-person.
☐	5.3.17 Are we getting the correct depth of insight and information from the business?	High level summaries and KPIs may not provide the depth to uncover small scale issues that are indicators of problems to come. However, large volumes of unfiltered static data create their own barriers to insight. The use of dynamic "what if" reports where summary data can be expanded/drilled into, may allow for more enquiring reviews by the board.
☐	5.3.18 How will the effectiveness of change management be reported to the board?	What are the measures needed to understand the effectiveness of change management? Although this is operational and not for the board to manage, it will be an initial indicator of any impacts to productivity due to the changes.
☐	5.3.19 Do our current policies provide the appropriate motivation and monitoring for the business we plan to be?	With the existing business operational framework in place, we may have policies that have been developed over many years. We need to consider how they align with the changes you are about to implement and update them if necessary.
☐	5.3.20 Do board members need to "walk the shop floor"?	Appropriate separation of the board and executive is important for the effective performance of the boards problem shaping role. However, during times of change the board may need to be more engaged with the business operations.

☒	Question	Why this matters
☐	5.3.21 Are we clear about who our key stakeholders are?	Aside from the shareholders, every company has a broader shareholder community. This can change over time as supply chains alter, target customers evolve etc. However, in times of transformation there can be significant changes to the stakeholder community.
☐	5.3.22 What posture will be projected for the digital transformation process?	There are many ways that the change process could be presented to stakeholders. The approach taken will need to be reflected in the overall communications narrative: • Nothing to see here, business as usual • We are doing something, but it is secret • Look what we are doing to reshape the business • etc
☐	5.3.23 Have we brought all stakeholders along for the ride?	In the absence of facts people tend to create the worst possible view of a situation. The board & executive need to set the narrative. It will enable the board and executive to have (some) control over how the message is interpreted. Ongoing communication and engagement will check how the narrative is landing and make adjustments as required.
☐	5.3.24 Have the key champions and detractors been identified?	During any period of change there will be champions and detractors. Identifying who these are will allow their enthusiasm or concerns to be managed. Sometimes those who are the biggest objectors initially can be the biggest supporters once their concerns are addressed.

☒	Question	Why this matters
☐	5.3.25 How will we monitor stakeholder sentiment?	Employees, customers and the broader stakeholder community will all be impacted by change. Monitoring their sentiment during the change process will help to highlight both positive and negative issues and allow for the appropriate action to take place.
☐	5.3.26 Have we considered social media and its impact on communication?	Both internal and external stakeholders have access to social media. How the narrative is managed on social media could impact the reputation of the business. It may be prudent to take an "if it can go wrong, it will go wrong" position and have the appropriate processes and responses considered in advance.
☐	5.3.27 Have we considered getting experts to manage our (social) media presence?	Undesired communications in the media (Social, new or other), whether from internal or external sources, can cause reputational damage. There may be a requirement to engage with external experts to assist with this.
☐	5.3.28 Do we have the skills to manage the change process internally?	If we are using an internal team for the change management process, we need to decide if our resources have the relevant skills to deliver the changes. • Has this been done before internally? • Was the project successful? • How was the change process measured? • How significant was the project compared to this one? Do they have the skills and understanding to manage a digital transformation project?

☒	Question	Why this matters
☐	5.3.29 How will we deal with the loss of undocumented intellectual property?	No matter how hard businesses try, much of their IP is held by staff rather than being formally documented. Loss of staff can lead to a potentially significant "brain drain". This can impact everything from the business culture to Enterprise Architecture (EA)[68].
☐	5.3.30 Have we considered how to deal with our technical debt?	The existing technology infrastructure is likely to have a level of technical debt[69] that increases costs over time e.g. maintaining customised code becomes more complex over time. Part of the justification for deploying a new technology infrastructure may be a reduction in the debt. This is discussed further in the Digital landscape section.
☐	5.3.31 What processes do we have in place to measure and report to the board whether a project is successful?	Having a consistent process for monitoring the progress of individual projects within the overall digital transformation program will provide the board with a higher level of insight and transparency.

---

[68] *https://en.wikipedia.org/wiki/Enterprise_architecture*
[69] *https://en.wikipedia.org/wiki/Technical_debt*

5.4 Business model and strategy

Digital Transformation is challenging us to ask hard questions about what type of business we are today and what we will look like in the future. The answers may not make us comfortable, but it is highly unlikely that our future self will look the same as we do today.

Figure 25 - Business model and strategy

There are many factors driving change, with the following being just a few of them:

- The increasing power of the knowledge rich customer
- Global supply chains
- The power of cloud computing to democratise access to enterprise grade services
- Barriers to entry for start-ups and new entrants being reduced
- Privacy and security challenges
- The growth in expectations for companies to have a clear social as well as commercial purpose.

If we refer to the Tricker model in chapter 2 (Board Skills & Focus), then in times of change, we need to shift the focus from predominantly inward to both inward and outward.

Technology in particular is allowing us to consider business models and strategies which may not have been previously viable. To take full advantage of this we may need to think further than just "outside the box" and into completely new spheres.

As discussed in Chapter 2 you cannot take your relevancy in the market for granted (Michael McQueens Relevancy Curve). Periodic transformation is essential and whilst the business models required may be new and/or not fully tried and tested, with the correct level of oversight and risk management they can create the competitive edge that sets the business up for a successful future.

> Technology is no longer just a tool; It is an integral part of your business operation. It removes the impedance to vision.

If we look at Kodak (Mui, 2012) as an example, there was no consideration for a change in their strategy until it was too late[70].

The executive knew it was going to be disrupted; they had already invented the digital camera internally in 1975. The corporate response to the invention was "But it was filmless photography, so management's reaction was, 'that's cute— but don't tell anyone about it...'"[71] (Deutsh, 2008).

In 1981 Kodak's head of market intelligence Vince Barabba (Barabba, et al., 2002) said it would take around ten years, so they had time to prepare. They did little to prepare for this disruption. They made exactly the mistake that George Eastman (its founder), avoided twice before. He moved from a profitable dry-plate business to film. He invested in color film even considering the fact it didn't measure up to black and white film quality. Even here Kodak was dominant. [72]

They were a market leader who did not believe they could or would be disrupted. By 1988, Kodak still hadn't realised they had lost the battle against digital photography. They didn't take any serious advantage of the opportunities to disrupt themselves.

---

[70] *https://www.forbes.com/sites/chunkamui/2012/01/18/how-kodak-failed/#2be305086f27*
[71] *http://www.nytimes.com/2008/05/02/technology/02kodak.html*
[72] *http://pubsonline.informs.org/doi/abs/10.1287/inte.32.1.20.18*

☒	Question	Why this matters
☐	5.4.1 Do we have a defined digital strategy for the next 3 to 5 years?	If the digital strategy is not formally defined and aligned to the timescales of the overarching business plan, then it is likely to be treated as a series of tactical activities rather than something that will drive long term value into the business. This will make it easier to prioritise funding, define the optimal delivery plan of the services and ultimately minimise the waste of funds
☐	5.4.2 Have we adopted a formal approach to analysing and documenting our revised strategy	Models allow us to express the constituents of the business model in a clear and concise method. These common models make it easier for others to understand and contribute. A few examples are: • Business model canvas[73] • Porter's 5 Forces[74] Blue Ocean Strategy[75]
☐	5.4.3 Is the Digital strategy agile enough to pivot and take advantage of new services & technologies?	The rate of change in the Information Technology and Communications sector means that new solutions and services are regularly becoming available. There is a balance that needs to be made so we don't keep jumping into new ideas, however the business may be able to gain significant advantage from some of these evolving technologies. An agile digital strategy will allow the company to take advantage of these technologies along the way?
☐	5.4.4 Is ongoing innovation a part of your strategy?	The rate of change in not just technology, but also the expectations of customers and society at large. They will require businesses to build innovation and entrepreneurship into the company culture.

---

[73] *https://en.wikipedia.org/wiki/Business_Model_Canvas*
[74] *https://en.wikipedia.org/wiki/Porter%27s_five_forces_analysis*
[75] *https://en.wikipedia.org/wiki/Blue_Ocean_Strategy*

☒	Question	Why this matters
☐	5.4.5 Does the structure of the organisation need to change to meet the new model?	An organisational restructure may be required. This will have implications both internally and externally It will require careful strategic change management.
☐	5.4.6 Does our core value proposition need to be updated?	This may seem an extreme step, however both macro and micro factors can fundamentally change the characteristics of business sectors. In the face of online retailers, traditional bricks and motor retailers are having to question where their real value to the customer lies.
☐	5.4.7 Does transformation result in the creation of a new venture?	The transformation may be sufficiently disruptive to justify the creation of a new business venture. This could be a new internal division or a completely new business. Lockheed Martin created their Skunk Works[76] division to create an environment where innovation could occur and "No mission was impossible".
☐	5.4.8 Does transformation lead to new or enhanced products and services?	Transformative thinking may create new products within the existing business or add new models around an existing one. Microsoft Office 365[77] was a radically new (subscription) model based on their existing Office client (Word, Excel etc) and server products (Exchange, SharePoint etc). A number of coffee shops have established a program for "suspended[78]" or "pay it forward" coffee to enhance their social purpose.

---

[76] https://www.lockheedmartin.com/en-us/who-we-are/business-areas/aeronautics/skunkworks.html
[77] https://www.office365.com/
[78] http://suspendedcoffees.com/

☒	Question	Why this matters
☐	5.4.9 Is transformation a catalyst for a full business renewal	In some cases, the transformation may be so disruptive that it prompts a fundamental business change and renewal. For example: [79] • Starbucks originally sold the espresso machines, not the coffee. • Twitter was originally a podcast subscription service
☐	5.4.10 Are our traditional strengths now weaknesses?	Skills, resources and ideas that have helped build the business to where it is today may now be the impediments to change going forward. For example: • On premises computer hardware in a cloud era • Staff used to monitor client equipment in an IoT era From assets that created barriers to entry they can become liabilities that reduce flexibility and increase costs.
☐	5.4.11 What do we do, or could we do, that would make the strengths of the competition irrelevant?	This is a core question asked in Blue Ocean Strategy[80]. We can spend a lot of time trying to be slightly better than our competitors in well-established areas, when all of us are already above the minimum level required by our customers.
☐	5.4.12 Can we remove areas of our offering and actually enhance customer value?	It may seem counter intuitive, but if a capability in your current offer adds a disproportionate cost or limits your ability to make it quicker/smaller/lighter etc then customers may be happy to lose one capability to gain the new benefit. This is another question posed in Blue Ocean Strategy.

[79] https://www.forbes.com/sites/jasonnazar/2013/10/08/14-famous-business-pivots/
[80] https://en.wikipedia.org/wiki/Blue_Ocean_Strategy

☒	Question	Why this matters
☐	5.4.13 Can existing resources be repurposed to drive new value?	Creative thinking may allow existing resources/systems to be used in different ways to drive new value without wholesale reinvestment. Direct Line insurance disrupted the UK insurance market by disintermediating the brokers. Initially this was done by simply allowing customers to call them directly via the telephone.
☐	5.4.14 Do existing resources have un-used or undervalued capabilities?	The complexity of IT systems can mean that there is functionality that is overlooked. There may also be enhanced capability available in upgrades that have not been implemented. Greater understanding and training could deliver enhanced capability without having to adopt new systems. For example, even with new solutions such as Microsoft Office 365, many of the included services such as SharePoint and Teams, are rarely used.
☐	5.4.15 Do our current products become services?	There has been a significant social shift to consumption economics[81] where products are not purchased upfront through CapEx budgets, but as ongoing OpEx subscriptions. Everything is now offered as a service XaaS. There are significant business model implications across every area of the business
☐	5.4.16 What are our existing competitors doing?	If one company in a sector is feeling the transformation pressure, then it is pretty certain others will be as well. Understanding whether the business is leading the pack or following will help to set the urgency of action. Note, just because competitors are not shouting about change, does not mean they are doing nothing. Digging for the truth may be required!

---

[81] *https://www.amazon.com/Consumption-Economics-New-Rules-Tech/dp/0984213031*

☒	Question	Why this matters
☐	5.4.17 How will the relationship with our customers change?	The bargaining power of customers has increased radically. They are demanding customer excellence based on their requirements, rather than a business's internal customer centric view. They may wish to engage through different channels or pay in different ways. The relationship may become more direct OR vice versa
☐	5.4.18 Do our customers see us as "One business" or multiple silos?	A businesses internal structures can result in customers seeing multiple different entities instead of a co-ordinated whole. This can result in strange behaviours from the customer perspective e.g. purchases from the one store (especially online) cannot be returned to another one. A true omni-channel[82] relationship can be complex internally, but it is what customers expect and "new" providers will deliver.
☐	5.4.19 Do we need to redefine who our target customers are?	Characteristics used to define target segments such as geographic, demographic, psychographic and behavioural can change over time. Segments may disappear, emerge or morph, creating new opportunities for those willing and able to adapt. For example, gin has transformed itself from "mother's favourite" to a trendy youth drink.
☐	5.4.20 Will our target market expand geographically?	Globalisation has created many growth opportunities. Technology has allowed increasingly effective engagement at distance and virtual offices to follow staff around the world. Logistical services are available to deliver products throughout the world at highly competitive costs.

---

[82] *https://en.wikipedia.org/wiki/Omnichannel*

☒	Question	Why this matters
☐	5.4.21 Do our support services need to "follow the sun"?	If you expand across geographies, then your support services will probably need to be available in local time zones.
☐	5.4.22 Are our sales activities increasingly at arm's length?	With online services the marketing and sales process may occur entirely at arm's length with not direct engagement. The first human contact could easily be within the Support organisation. This may require a review of the "sales skills" with the support team and the clarification of the role of the sales team.
☐	5.4.23 Have we tested the new or changing market appropriately?	Looking at change internally for a business is important. It is even more imperative to make sure the new offerings are appropriate for the target market, as this will be one of the primary determining factors between success and failure.
☐	5.4.24 Have we validated the value and relevancy of our existing supplier relationships?	Good relationships with suppliers can take time and trust to build. If these suppliers are also transforming, then their value may continue or even be enhanced. However, if they are resisting change or heading in a different direction then their relevancy can quickly disappear.
☐	5.4.25 Have we analysed the new suppliers entering the market?	Most of the time new suppliers offer evolutionary change with a slightly better capability, slightly improved price point etc. However, sometimes new suppliers can fundamentally change the game. New materials or manufacturing techniques can create new possibilities for designing, building or pricing offerings. Thinking about the compromises made to current offerings because of current supplier constraints, can help give focus to the analysis. However, new capabilities can come from left field, so it is important to keep an open mind.

☒	Question	Why this matters
☐	5.4.26 How could emerging products or services replace our current offerings?	Emerging products can totally replace even dominant offerings. The digital camera has effectively replaced film-based cameras and streaming content services such as Netflix have replaced businesses such as Blockbuster. Self-driving cars and drones have the potential to create fundamental disruption in the transportation and logistics business in the near to mid future.
☐	5.4.27 Have we analysed the new competitors entering our market?	It can be easy to miss or ignore new entrants to a market. Their offerings are often inferior to the current market leaders (using the established measures), but they offer capabilities that deliver new outcomes. If these are aligned to outcomes and customer values, then they will be a threat. IBM failed to recognise the threat posed by Microsoft and the PC. Microsoft in turn failed to recognise the threat of Apple and the mobile phone or Amazon Web Services and Cloud Services
☐	5.4.28 Has our budget approach changed to support an agile business approach?	The market is being driven by faster cycles of innovation. Annual budgets, once set, have limited flexibility and may no longer be fit for purpose. This is not about abandoning budgeting rigour, but rather about including processes that allow for agility.
☐	5.4.29 Does our revenue flow change?	One of the major impacts of digital transformation can be a shift from upfront/CapEx revenue to recurring/subscription/OpEx. There can be implications across the whole business including financial (revenue recognition, cash flow etc), cultural (sales skills and compensation) and systems (processing invoices changes from an annual basis to every month, with corresponding resources in AR).

X	Question	Why this matters
☐	5.4.30 How will our cost structures change?	The cost structures within the business change radically and require new KPIs and or monitoring. There may be less fixed and more variable costs. There may be more contract rather than permanent staff. We may gain or lose volume discounts as suppliers change.
☐	5.4.31 Does your business provide post-sales support to your customers?	Technology enables automation of post-sales support and service. Internet connected instrumentation and equipment can automatically identify maintenance issues and alert the vendor to send service staff to resolve the issue (e.g. an elevator that has a vibration sensor which indicates one of its bearings is at risk of imminent failure). This can provide a point of differentiation for customers.
☐	5.4.32 Does your business provide consumables that need to be regularly replenished for your customers?	Technology such as IoT and AI enables supply chain automation (fleet management, route optimization, warehouse inventory), semi-automation and therefore increased replenishment velocity.
☐	5.4.33 Do the products you sell have a software component?	Remote management enables regular over-the-air technology updates which means the life cycle of the product extends and new capabilities can be delivered as you go. It also potentially represents a decrease in services activities as more issues may be solved remotely.

☒	Question	Why this matters
☐	5.4.34 How will selling outcomes impact your business risk?	Selling outcomes changes the relationship with customers. It is likely that you will have a deeper engagement with the customer which can reduce risk. However, you will also have a greater responsibility for delivering the promised business outcomes.
☐	5.4.35 Will increased customer intimacy require new business processes?	As technology allows vendors to connect directly to customers and understand them better, it also means that vendors will need to change their business processes to support more customer interaction. For example, when Microsoft moved from selling Office to selling Office 365 online they had to greatly expand their call centres and customer service capabilities to support the increased level of direct customer interaction these new business models would bring.
☐	5.4.36 Does the increased responsiveness that real time telemetry of the product provides represent a differentiator for your customers?	Technology may increase the speed at which you get information from your customers. But unless your business processes adapt to take advantage of that speed, your customers may end up becoming disappointed rather than excited. For example, an elevator manufacturer that provides real time telemetry indicating that an elevator is in imminent risk of failure may only frustrate customers if they don't provide 24/7 support and the elevator breaks down before this increased level of information can be taken advantage of.

☒	Question	Why this matters
☐	5.4.37 Can increased information about your customers' usage patterns allow you to understand them better and provide more tailored service offerings?	Technology such as IoT and AI can provide greater insights into your customers. Using this data to better understand them may enable you to offer more tailored service offerings through different business models. This can not only increase customer satisfaction and hence customer loyalty; the data can be used for Machine Learning and AI training.
☐	5.4.38 With increased information can your processes be more automated?	A core part of Digital Transformation is the transition of human resources into higher value-added roles. Technology can facilitate greater process automation and therefore free up human resources.
☐	5.4.39 What changes will affect people & processes?	When carrying out a digital transformation project, there is a significant amount of change which affects people and process. With this comes substantial training for the operators and especially the internal & external stakeholders.
☐	5.4.40 Have we planned for the change in support and operational resources	When moving from an infrastructure model to a Cloud or SaaS model, there is a requirement to consider a change in skill requirements. Have we considered plans for the employees? • Retraining • Redundancies Hiring a new skillset
☐	5.4.41 Have we considered the short-term productivity implications?	With any change there is a period of adaptation and adoption. During this period productivity is likely to dip. Allowance may need to be made for longer process/delivery/response time etc. There may be a short term need for additional resources.

☒	Question	Why this matters
☐	5.4.42 Do we have a plans to retrain and reskill existing staff?	Typically, a large part of the enterprise architecture team is technology focused around infrastructure. These team members would need reskilling focusing on cloud services, application development, Machine Learning, Data analytics and IoT.
☐	5.4.43 Do we have plans to hire staff with new skills?	We need to assess the current skillset of our employees relating to the expected changes, so we understand the requirements to manage the processes for employee re skilling, hiring or retrenchment. This doesn't sound very difficult at the outset; however, if the process is not managed effectively, it can result in significant losses to productivity, waste and project failure
☐	5.4.44 Do we have plans to manage the retrenchment of staff?	Does the organisation have the capability to manage the processes for employee retrenchment? This can be a very delicate process and needs to be managed effectively to reduce the impact on the business and the remaining employees.

Chapter

Marketplace Questions

Change is the only constant in life

Heraclitus of Ephesus (c. 500 BCE)

WE live in an increasing connected world, both as individuals and businesses. The previous chapter was focused on internal questions. In this chapter we consider the questions that are influenced by the external marketplace in which we operate.

We are not totally in control of our own destiny as we are impacted by the actions of others as much as we can impact them. With social media access and the "24 hour news", organisations are under continual scrutiny, leading to a higher level of transparency.

The rise of language such as "the purpose motive" and "profit for purpose" demonstrates that the broader stakeholder ecosystem is influenced by how organisations engage in this increasingly complex marketplace.

6.1 Supply chain

Supply chains are changing. There is a fundamental shift from broadly linear relationships to more complex ecosystems where roles are more fluid. Buyers can create IP and become suppliers and vice versa.

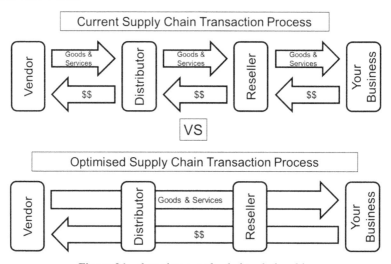

Figure 26 - changing supply chain relationships

Also, the shift to subscription services is moving the place of value exchange. Previously goods were sold from one stage of the supply chain to the next with risk transferring at the same time. Ultimately the end customer was left owning the risk (buyer beware). With subscription services the customer can choose to "walk away" and hence the risk remains within the supply chain. (supplier beware).

Creating efficiency within these complex ecosystems requires the exchange of information, which in turn means standards and agreed operating processes across organisations. The downside of this connected supply chain is that we are highly reliant on others. If a supplier leaves or goes bust, there can be a complex process to find a new supplier that not only meets the quality requirements, but can also support the standards that allow them to integrate

How sustainable Is your supply chain? Are you part of another organisations supply chain or they are part of yours? Are you part of one or many supply chains?

Be aware of where you fit and how you can make sure you are key to delivering better value through automation.

☒	Question	Why this matters
☐	6.1.1 Have we communicated our strategy for change to our supply chain?	We are about to go through a digital transformation of your organisation. There would be significant changes to our business from a technology perspective. Have we spoken to your supply chain to understand if they have any projects or changes which will impact our project?
☐	6.1.2 Have we done an audit of our supplier relationships?	Over time the number of suppliers can simply grow, with it being easier to maintain the status quo. Transformation can be an opportunity for consolidation. An audit of suppliers will identify those that are core and those that are peripheral. Some may also reduce in importance in the shift from the old to the new.
☐	6.1.3 Do critical partners share your vision for change?	The priorities of one company may not be those of another. A supplier may be focused on protecting their existing revenue streams and not yet ready to engage in transformation themselves. Or they may have a different view on the approach or technology involved in transformation. Better to find this out early and part as friends.
☐	6.1.4 Is secrecy during the transformation process possible or desirable?	Careful consideration is required around the practicality of maintaining secrecy in a "social media" world with multiple parties. Also, whether secrecy is desirable. Customers may want changes, but if they are not aware of what is happening, they may look for somebody else.
☐	6.1.5 Do all parties have a common understanding of disclosure obligations and implications?	If information is going to be shared do all parties have a common understanding of what is acceptable and the implications for other parties. One person's humour is another's reputational damage.

☒	Question	Why this matters
☐	6.1.6 Does critical IP need to be shared with 3rd parties to deliver transformation?	This could be to support the work of a delivery partner e.g. integration. It may be a requirement when engaging in an overseas JV e.g. China.
☐	6.1.7 Will partners in our supply chain be able to support our organisation in its new form?	Changes both organisationally and technologically may alter the way that external parties interact with you. Suppliers may make commitments to providing capabilities they don't currently offer or have the necessary skills to offer. It could land you in a position where your processes and security are compromised.
☐	6.1.8 How would we deal with using a start-up organisation in critical areas of transformation?	On one hand they are a new organisation. On the other hand, some of the older organisations don't have the same forethought relating to current and future business ideas and models. This is a risk management exercise which relates back to the board's appetite for risk.
☐	6.1.9 Would there be any ancillary benefits of using a start-up?	Taking the risks of using product from a start-up into account. There may be other benefits you could take advantage of such as marketing, advertising and case studies.
☐	6.1.10 Would there be government grants available for the use of the technology from the start-up?	There are several government initiatives which are driving industry, with these come with grants for investing in the use of some new leading and bleeding edge technologies. Would this assist to mitigate some of the risk associated with using specialist services or technology from a start-up?

☒	Question	Why this matters
☐	6.1.11 Are contracts aligned throughout our supply chain?	We are aggregating third party services to deliver a service to our clients. Do we have the appropriate back to back service contracts in place, where the supplier has committed to deliver at least the minimum service levels and availability we have negotiated with your clients? It's not a good idea to procure a service with a service level of 99.00% uptime and resell it as a service with 99.99% uptime
☐	6.1.12 Who is reviewing and updating our supply chain contracts?	There are two aspects to the supply chain contract, which need to be addressed: Legal: This should be reviewed by a lawyer who understands the implications of data breaches and the impact to your business. A commercial lawyer with no experience with these types of contracts may not be the most appropriate for this. Technical: This should be reviewed by a legal team who has experience with these documents as they can be very ambiguous or have hidden costs which will only come to light after the contract has started and can significantly change the paradigm of the agreement. These include cyber and data security.
☐	6.1.13 Can suppliers grow to meet our requirements?	Transformation may significantly alter the scope of an organisation. This could involve increased customer numbers, expansion into overseas markets or extended service hours.
☐	6.1.14 Should we consider investing in our supplier's IT infrastructure?	Sharing, supporting, funding or even mandating the rollout of technology and infrastructure within your supply chain may be necessary to accelerate the benefit capture.

☒	Question	Why this matters
☐	6.1.15 What processes are in place to monitor the overseas elements of our supply chain?	Measuring and monitoring process and quality overseas, may create additional overheads. This could be due to supplier and/or delivery partners.
☐	6.1.16 Do we, or our suppliers have mechanisms in place to report service levels?	If they are uncomfortable with this, then you need to question their confidence that they can hit their service level agreement (SLA) targets. You should also have a mechanism to measure their SLAs and a process internally to trigger alerts. Don't expect the supplier to have the monitoring in place.
☐	6.1.17 Do partners need updated or new certifications?	The increased use of technology may require enhanced or additional certifications. E.g. ISO 9001 may need to be supplemented with ISO 270001.
☐	6.1.18 Are the employees of the outsourced partner appropriately certified?	If you are planning on aggregating services to your customers. You may want to make sure the organisation providing those services are appropriately certified to reduce risk.

6.2 Accountability and Legal

This section specifically relates to responsibility. In some ways it is perceived as the negative aspect of the conversation however it is the straight-talking bit where everybody puts skin in the game to makes sure the transformation is successful.

It is about responsibility and intention, not about blame and mitigation of personal risk. When you agree to procure services from another organisation the onus of responsibility for these services, still resides within your organisation. It is up to your organisation to make sure the appropriate levels of service are delivered.

The idea of accountability is somewhat abstract in this context as the organisation can hold the services organisation accountable for any failures in service. However, your organisation itself is ultimately responsible to its customers.

Outsourcing of your services does not abdicate your organisation's accountability of the service levels delivered to your customers.

This is also key to the appropriate management of security for your services. It is ultimately the board's responsibility to make sure customer information and data is secured appropriately. With this in mind, there is a requirement for scrutiny of any organisations or customers in your supply chain.

Figure 27 - Accountability and legal

Please note, we are not lawyers and hence all normal caveats apply. The questions in this section (and the others) are simply a reflection of the experiences we have gained during our own transformation journeys.

☒	Question	Why this matters
☐	6.2.1 Does our digital/business transformation lead to a broader social accountability?	The purpose of transformation is to enhance the future value of the business. However, this may have consequences beyond the desired fiscal success. Will digital workers & AI replace "skilled workers" such as lawyers. If so, where will the junior lawyers learn their skills to become experts? If we can offshore or work remotely, what are the impacts on the current and future local communities? Transformation creates an opportunity to consider enhanced value from both a fiscal and social perspective. "The business of business is to make the world a better place[83]"
☐	6.2.2 Do we have a unionized workforce?	Job changes due to digital transformation, including enhanced employee monitoring and possible workforce reductions or redeployment, may become the cause of concern with your unions. Early communications will be key.
☐	6.2.3 Do our transformation plans need to be notified to regulatory agencies?	You may have obligations to notify government oversite organisations such as APRA, ASIC, RBA, CFR, ACCC of any changes you may be undertaking?
☐	6.2.4 Do our transformation plans mean we need to report to new agencies?	There may be obligations to inform and provide ongoing reporting, to government oversite organisations, such as APRA of any changes being undertaken.

☒	Question	Why this matters
☐	6.2.5 Will government regulators establish new agencies or regulations that impact digital transformation?	Much of government legislation related to Digital Transformation is still in its infancy. However, there is a growing recognition that the impact of technology, and regulation is beginning to be enacted. Being engaged with the bodies that are shaping this emerging legislation could be a positive investment. With knowledge of what is coming, positive and planned steps forward can be taken.
☐	6.2.6 Are our digital transformation plans ahead of current legislation?	Being on the leading edge can mean operating in an unregulated space. This can create opportunities to be part of defining the future and establishing competitive advantage. However, just because something can be done, doesn't necessarily mean it is ethically acceptable.
☐	6.2.7 Are we subject to data privacy legislation such as GDPR[84]?	Governments around the world are implementing increasing levels of legislation to protect the privacy and management of "personal" data. An example of this is the GDPR in Europe (with an intent to have a global reach), and the Notifiable Data Breach Scheme in Australia[85].
☐	6.2.8 Where does accountability sit when services are outsourced to external parties?	Using an external organisation to deliver services does not necessarily allow the business to abdicate responsibility/ownership. Being clear about the responsibilities in this extended and diversified business model will be critical to managing risks.

---

[84] *https://gdpr-info.eu/*
[85] *https://www.oaic.gov.au/privacy-law/privacy-act/notifiable-data-breaches-scheme*

☒	Question	Why this matters
☐	6.2.9 Will Director liability change due to the increase of security issues?	In recent cyber-attacks, hackers used co-opted IoT devices to launch attacks against other third parties. There is talk of legislation to make companies responsible if the IoT devices they own are used to launch attacks against other third parties. This is just one example of increased scrutiny of security implications for technology to be implemented. Cyber insurance may need to be added to the organisation's insurance requirements.
☐	6.2.10 Will Director liability change due to privacy issues?	New privacy legislation increases the responsibility of companies with the directors ultimately owning the responsibility regarding the private data they collect from 3rd parties. The increase in data collected about customers may increase the liability for company directors, however, addressing these issues could create a positive differentiator for you within your customer base.
☐	6.2.11 Do Director and Officer insurances provide appropriate cover for the emerging technology risks?	Existing policies may not have had their wording updated to reflect the growing reliance on technology and the related cyber risks. As an example, cover may be limited to specific geographies (in country). This may have been acceptable previously with on-premises deployments, but now that cloud services can be delivered from any and sometimes multiple global locations, this will be required to change.

☒	Question	Why this matters
☐	6.2.12 Will customers have concerns regarding the data collected about them?	When asked, most people want increased levels of privacy even though they will take little action to ensure their own privacy. This is called the Privacy Paradox. Your customers may start questioning you about your products and services because of the data you are capturing about them. Being clear about how you use the data and how you meet or exceed compliance rules will be important. Equally showing how you use the data to provide benefits for the customer will help them see the benefits, not just risks.
☐	6.2.13 Will supply chain partners have concerns with data collected about them or shared customers?	Partners may be concerned about the risk of being disintermediated and ultimately being put out of business. Proactive discussions with partners will aid in the transition.
☐	6.2.14 How does liability change due to the increased connectivity of organisations to the internet?	In a recent Denial of Service attack, simple consumer devices connected to the internet were co-opted to launch a large internet attack on commercial web sites. The consumers who owned these devices largely did not know that their devices had been co-opted. There is the possibility that equipment your company owns, connected to the internet, could be used to launch an attack on a third party. A clear risk assessment and appropriate mitigation strategies can enhance your reputation for good governance and outweigh any potential for increased liability.

☒	Question	Why this matters
☐	6.2.15 How will a move from product to outcome-based services impact business risk?	In the move to "as-a-Service" business models the IT industry ended up taking on the risk of ensuring uptime on the solutions they were providing, which included guarantees and associated penalty clauses in contracts. This meant that some risk and the responsibility for success was transferred from the customer to the vendor. Invariably the customer ended up paying more to the vendor for taking on this risk and there was increased customer lock-in. There are benefits and risks to both parties however, if managed there is enhanced shareholder value for all.
☐	6.2.16 Is the IP created during the transformation process appropriately protected?	If multiple parties are working on the leading edge of business and technology, it is possible that IP will be created. Establishing who owns what in advance will reduce the chance for disputes later.
☐	6.2.17 What SLA's are in place?	The SLA (Service Level Agreement) is the basis for the provisioning of the service and it is critical that it reflects the real-world requirements of the business and provides comfort that these requirements will be met. In our experience there is a clear link between the quality of a supplier's operational procedures and security policies and the quality of their SLA's. Take a hard look at the SLAs against the business requirements.

☒	Question	Why this matters
☐	6.2.18 What level of SLA do you really need?	Just because a vendor offers an option for 99.999% uptime, does not mean it is necessary (and prices increase rapidly as you add 9s!!. Apparently impressive SLA's can be misleading. 99.999% availability (referred to as "five nines"[86] and seen by many as the gold standard for availability) = 5.26 minutes per year of downtime, is impressive. However, if there are "allowed exclusions" (say 1am to 3am) every day then this adds 730 hours of service unavailability within the SLA. If you are a purely 9 to 5 business, then this may appear to be irrelevant. But what happens if you have clients (maybe overseas) who wish to engage with you out of your local hours. When (not if) incidents occur, then response times may need to vary depending on the severity of the outage, which in turn may vary depending on whether it is a peak period, and this may vary by location.
☐	6.2.19 Is the SLA worth the paper it is written on?	It does not matter how impressive the SLA appears, if there is no consequence on the provider for failure to deliver on the promises. Penalties should reflect the severity of the business impact. However, in our experience most SLAs are very conservative, typically limited, to little more than "what you have already paid for the service", with no "consequential damages". Be clear about what real world remedies are available for service provider failures.

☒	Question	Why this matters
☐	6.2.20 Are the exceptions or exclusions embedded in the contract reasonable?	Service providers will add exemption, exclusion or "reasonable use" clauses to protect themselves. These maybe for "unreasonable" or "unforeseen" uses of the service e.g. using a capability in an unplanned, or even illegal way. It is important to understand these and ensure that they are not central to the capability you are expecting from the service. The impact could be a lack of service or significantly higher than expected costs.
☐	6.2.21 What "transfer of rights" are in the contract?	Many Cloud Computing vendors will have an exit strategy based on being purchased by a bigger player. To ensure that this is easy for the purchaser they may include some form of right to pass on (novate) contracts. This ensures continuity of service and could have additional benefits e.g. a larger player providing greater funding and a wider range of services and facilities. However, this may result in work or challenges for us: • Do we need to "assess the risk" of the new owner? • Is the new owner going to consolidate the service in a new data centre that may be out of our geography and create data ownership issues? The new owner may present issues from a political, ethical, or even legal perspective?

☒	Question	Why this matters
☐	6.2.22 Have we considered the implications of the termination clause?	Both parties must have options to terminate the agreement however they should be balanced. What notice periods are required, are they "without cause"? Can the service provider simply stop offering the service? If it is an overseas provider are there arbitration services and if so, where are they based?
☐	6.2.23 Is there a clearly defined dispute management process?	In the event of a dispute, does the contract help us get what we need? These are standard in most contracts; however, the global nature of the technology business means that, the vendor and/or the services they are delivering may be in another country. The contract may be governed by overseas laws and your ability to vary this may be limited, even if you are a large company. This can impact the viability of litigation even if you are in the right. If the services are critical to your business then far better to "plan for the divorce, not the honeymoon". Disputes can also go both ways; the vendor may decide that they have a dispute with you. What is the notification period for remedy and are there any "3 strikes and you are out" clauses? There should be an "ultimate authority" that can be used to resolve disputes, but be careful to ensure they are a credible organization?

☒	Question	Why this matters
☐	6.2.24 In the event of departure (friendly or otherwise) is there sufficient time and support to migrate to a new service?	Whether through dispute, termination or agreed departure, there will probably be a requirement to migrate to a replacement service. The contract should include provisions for sufficient time and support from the service provider to allow this to be a graceful process.
☐	6.2.25 How is "data ownership" handled in the supplier's contract?	We need to understand how our data is handled and managed, what the contractual responsibilities are, relating to the ownership and the way our data is handled. • What provisions are in our contract for data ownership? • What rights do we have during the contract? • What happens at the end of the contract or if we breach any terms? • How do we get copies and in what formats? • What rights has the vendor included to allow them to handle our data e.g. for backups? • The data should always be ours, but out of sight should not be out of mind. Be clear about our rights to copies of the data to store our self, even if this is a chargeable service. • What happens if the vendor goes out of business, how quickly can we have a backup of our data so we can find another service vendor, and in what formats. Even if we have a copy of the data, do we need proprietary tools that only the vendor has access to in order to read the data?

☒	Question	Why this matters
☐	6.2.26 What are our rights to use the data we collect?	Our right to use the data that we collect needs to be clearly established. For "in-house" data this may be straight forward. But where it is "external", especially where people and privacy are concerned, this may not be as straight forward. People are giving very personal health data to organizations like FitBit with little thought for the future use. We need to consider how we would be positioned both legally and ethically.
☐	6.2.27 Are there geographical implications in the contract?	Depending on the location of the data centre the applicable legislation and the rights of the local authorities will vary e.g. the rights to access data within the data centre. Reciprocal arrangements may be in place between governments, that could enhance or reduce your protections.
☐	6.2.28 Do contracts we have with our customers either explicitly or implicitly set restrictions on the geographic location of data storage?	This may be a deliberate requirement e.g. storage of government data in-country. Or it could be a legacy of contracts that were not written with the "cloud" in mind. You may be able to negotiate changes with customers, but failure to do so could put you in breach with potentially damaging implications both financially and reputationally.
☐	6.2.29 Do contracts we have with our customers either explicitly or implicitly set data retention requirements?	There may be data retention requirements that you have not had to think about when you stored everything in your own infrastructure. However, the chosen service provider may have a retention period that is incompatible with your requirements. Extending this may be part of their "premium" service.

☒	Question	Why this matters
☐	6.2.30 What is the legal jurisdiction of the contract?	Our organization may be based in Australia, using a service in the UK, provided by an organisation based in France. Some providers offer a single contract globally with a single legal jurisdiction, others offer contracts tailored to the region of use. It is important to be clear about the implications, as it may be difficult to gain access to legal representation services in North Korea!!!!
☐	6.2.31 How do we terminate the service?	Even if everything has gone to plan and the service has met our needs, at some point we may wish to leave the service. It is important to agree up front how this will work. • How do we get copies of our data? • What happens to our data after we leave? • What support will the vendor provide to assist in our planned departure? • Are there any costs for this? etc.
☐	6.2.32 What are the exit terms in the contract?	Separate from termination, there may be reasons to exit from a service. There may be a lock-in clause, which expects our organisation to meet specified payment obligations or stating our organisation can leave whenever we want but apply exorbitant penalty rates as we withdraw from their services. There is greater power to deal with this during the negotiation phase than after.

☒	Question	Why this matters
☐	6.2.33 What is our liability if something goes wrong?	Questions about liability are asked in business all the time however, technology is expanding the scope. Depending on our industry, new exposures will emerge, for example: • Who is responsible if a driverless car has an accident – the driver or the manufacturer? • Who is responsible if a webcam is hacked and in turn is used to hack others? What happens if a bad decision is made based on data from the use of 3rd party data?
☐	6.2.34 Are there any "Step in" rights within the contract?	Are there rights that allow a 3rd party to "step in" and run the business in the event the supplier has difficulties? The business impact and the difficulty of transferring to another supplier will determine how important this is. This is amplified if the supplier uses a unique proprietary technology or service.

6.3 Digital Transformation Technology Partners

Digital Transformation of a business is not just replacing a few systems and full speed ahead, it is a significant project requiring forethought, planning and finesse. It does not only affect internal staff, but customers, supply chain and other external stakeholders.

Figure 28 - Digital Transformation Technology Partners

The technology partners selected to work on this project will be critical to a successful outcome. There may be comfort in working with existing suppliers or selecting a large partner however, the best skills may reside in smaller, start-up businesses, which can bring a significantly different relationship dynamic.

☒	Question	Why this matters
☐	6.3.1 Where is the partners vision, mission, focus?	Unless the partners vision for transformation is aligned, and support is clear from the executive level, then the challenges of change will be magnified. There will be problems along the way and if the project is not strategic for the partner then they may cut their losses and run.
☐	6.3.2 What is the unique/ critical value-add that the partner offers?	Being clear about the unique value the partner brings will assist in best utilising their resources, where other external parties fit-in and what needs to be done internally. It also helps to understand that the risks associated with using the partner and hence what mitigation strategies are required. (They may be the only supplier of a product or have unique IP that they bring.)
☐	6.3.3 What level of questioning and due diligence did the partner carry out up-front?	There are risks with any transformation project and the partner should be asking challenging questions, that check the executive support, budget coverage (especially contingency), strategic outcomes etc. so they can have confidence in the project success. A lack of knowledge could lead to a "make promises, close the deal and worry about details later" attitude.
☐	6.3.4 What experience does the partner have **inside** our industry?	Digital transformation is about business transformation and the partners domain expertise, not just their technology skills, but their business skills will be extremely valuable.
☐	6.3.5 What experience does the partner have **outside** our industry?	Disruption can often have its genesis from change in other industry sectors. A valuable partner will be able to bring these insights to the project.

☒	Question	Why this matters
☐	6.3.6 Is the partner offering products or an outcome?	This will reveal the level of commitment to the ultimate achievement of the desired outcomes. If the outcome is a parcel delivered in New York tomorrow before 9am, be clear about whether the partner: • provides the trucks, logistics software etc but they are not responsible for making it all work together and ultimately delivering the parcel • promises to deliver the parcel by 9am and manages the "how this happens" themselves. Being clear, will help clarify how much and what effort and responsibility is held by each party.
☐	6.3.7 What levels of business technology R&D does the partner engage in?	Partners should ideally have formally allocated research and development budgets (both money and time) and this should cover technology AND business.
☐	6.3.8 Does the partner belong to relevant industry bodies (business or technology)?	Both contributing to and receiving feedback from industry bodies is a great way for the partner to demonstrate their commitment to ongoing R&D.
☐	6.3.9 Does the partner have experience in our existing/ legacy systems?	Even though the transformation is likely to be about new systems and services, the data will probably reside in legacy systems. Migrating the data will be a key activity and vastly simplified if the partner has experience in both old and new systems.
☐	6.3.10 Can the partner offer references that are willing to discuss their experiences?	Case studies are one thing, but a direct conversation with a previous customer can be very revealing. The partner may not have a perfect match, but a history of "meeting their promises", flexibility etc with related projects, will still have great value.

☒	Question	Why this matters
☐	6.3.11 What evidence of a proven SLA track record is available?	Whilst past performance is no guarantee of future performance, a good track record can provide confidence. SLA's are a critical measure and a proven track record, even in other areas, is important. Also, when issues do occur, how they are researched and reported on, will provide an insight into the importance the partner places on SLA's.
☐	6.3.12 What information does the partner provide to allow their performance to be monitored?	There is an argument that if you outsource an activity to a partner, then they should just be left to get on with it. However, our experience is that early identification and open discussion of activities that are slipping, is a critical aspect of successful projects. If this is true, then the greater the transparency from the partner the better.
☐	6.3.13 Does the partner have relevant independent/ industry certifications?	Although standards that are directly applicable to the area of transformation may not yet exist, a partner's broader commitment to independent assessment is a positive indicator of their overall attitude. These may be for people - certified vendor specialist, the offering - HIPPA compliance, or the company as a whole - ISO 9001.
☐	6.3.14 Does the partner have the required geographic reach, and can they expand?	A local/smaller/start-up partner may have the perfect skills, but there may be limitations on their ability to expand with you. This could be development and deployment skills, overseas offices, follow the sun support etc. This should not be a blocker to using them, but awareness will provide visibility as to where their skills should be focused, or where additional relationships need to be built. The partner may be able to do this through their own extended network.

☒	Question	Why this matters
☐	6.3.15 How precise is the Statement of Work?	A balance needs to be achieved in a SoW so it contains enough detail to give confidence/comfort, but also enough flexibility to manage the inevitable changes required on the journey.
☐	6.3.16 What handover is provided at the end of the project by the partner?	Agreeing on the level of documentation and knowledge transfer required, both during and at the end of the project, will help to manage the risks of, amongst other things: • "key man" • lost IP • supplier lock-in
☐	6.3.17 If the partner is a vendor, do they have a user group?	Vendors user groups are often a great way to gain real world insights into the business and the offerings. Things to consider are: • How big/many attendees • How often do they meet • Are they rubber stamp affairs or genuine listening sessions.
☐	6.3.18 What is the partners financial position and backing?	Start-ups may have significant backing; established players may have cash flow constraints. Being aware of how deep the partners pockets are will help manage the inevitable "money issues" that arise throughout a project.
☐	6.3.19 How important is this project to the partner?	Hight importance will prioritise, resources, executive support etc. and provide a strong win-win position on project success. Conversely, if this is a "bet the business" project for the partner, then it may introduce project risks that need to be managed.

☒	Question	Why this matters
☐	6.3.20 What marketing benefits are there from working with the partner?	The project may confer credibility on the partner, and they may be keen to work on joint marketing collateral. Be clear in advance about any limitations on what can be shared, or conversely how "big" you both want to go. Conversely the partner involvement may provide credibility to the project and potential exposure that would otherwise be unavailable (e.g. a case study at a vendors annual worldwide conference)

Chapter

Digital Landscape Questions

We cannot solve our problems with the same thinking we used when we created them

Albert Einstein (Theoretical Physicist. 1879 – 1955)

A S discussed in the opening chapters, business and cultural change are critical aspects of any Digital Transformation project. The questions related to these areas have been covered in the previous two chapters. Now it is time to explore the technology questions.

This is NOT about being technical.

A Director does not need to be an accountant or a lawyer to be informed about financial and legal matters.

In the same way, this chapter is intended to create awareness that allows a Director to ask informed questions and to effectively enquire about technology, without being a technical guru.

The following diagram provides a visual representation of some of the areas that need to be considered.

This may appear overwhelming so to simplify things, we have broken this down into 3 areas:

- starting with the high level architectural questions
- then getting deeper into the technology (but remember this is about awareness, not being a techie)

- finally, an area of increasing concern for Directors, (Cyber) security and privacy.

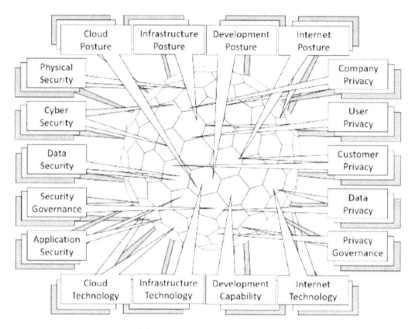

Figure 29 - Digital landscape

> "The world is being re-shaped by the convergence of social, mobile, cloud, big data, community and other powerful forces. The combination of these technologies unlocks an incredible opportunity to connect everything together in a new way and is dramatically transforming the way we live and work."
>
> **Marc Benioff, Founder and CEO, Salesforce**

7.1 Asking the Big High-level questions

It can be tempting, especially when there are disruptive pressures, to dive in and just start solving high priority issues. All too often service providers or vendors, will suggest it is easy to solve a problem now, if only you implement their X, Y or Z.

The role of the director is to think about shaping before solving.

"Without strategy, execution is aimless. Without execution, strategy is useless." Morris Chang

If we wish to shape the outcome then, we need to understand at a high level, where we currently are, and the strategic direction we want technology to take us.

As an example, there may be underutilised skills, capabilities or systems within the business that could deliver change without additional investment. Conversely, relying on current skills and/or systems, even if used more effectively, may re-enforce existing processes and inhibit more innovative approaches that could deliver fundamental change in process, customer interaction etc.

Is there enough benefit from a custom developed solution, to justify the costs and time required, or does the speed of deploying a standard, configured solution offer greater benefits?

The questions in this section are intended to strip back these outer layers, to help you shape "where you ought to go from here" and provide context to the deeper technology questions that come next.

Figure 30 - The high level questions

☒	Question	Why this matters
☐	7.1.1 How focused are the IT team on the end user experience?	The traditional complexity of technology has meant that simply ensuring systems work has been enough, however one of the fundamental drivers for digital transformation is the rising expectation of users both internally and externally, for systems and processes, that are focused on their user experience. Without this shift in focus there is a high likelihood of poor user adoption and hence project risk.
☐	7.1.2 Do we have sufficient budget to deliver the training required to maximise the benefits from the new systems and processes?	With the implementation of new applications and technologies, there is a requirement for user and operator training as part of the change process. Without this in place, and the appropriate support, the service levels will not be sustainable, the on flow of this is loss of productivity or clients, or both.
☐	7.1.3 Have we carried out an audit of our current systems?	Companies typically have multiple systems within their business and significant existing infrastructure. The business needs to confirm whether existing systems need to co-exist with new technologies and if so, what it will take to achieve this. The existing business systems may provide a head start, OR they may be a blocker. It is better to invest the time early on, rather than find out later.
☐	7.1.4 Is there unused/ underused capability in existing systems?	The functionality of IT systems is typically enhanced by the supplier in each new release. These existing systems may therefore have capabilities, that if fully utilised, could meet the requirements of the digital transformation project, however, be careful that this "re-use" does not compromise the greater future good.

☒	Question	Why this matters
☐	7.1.5 Have we completed a systems risk analysis from a business perspective?	Having a detailed understanding of the risks associated with IT systems from a business perspective (likelihood and impact), it is essential to ensure that the appropriate mitigation strategies are implemented. For example, the appropriate mitigation for a low likelihood, but high impact scenario may be insurance rather than a high cost technology solution.
☐	7.1.6 Will shadow IT have an impact on the project?	Shadow IT are services procured by business teams, bypassing corporate IT. This may be the defacto, but unknown way, that business units are able to bypass IT procurement processes and application scrutiny to get quicker results with new applications. There needs to be a consideration given to the possible impact this may have on the project and transformation?
☐	7.1.7 How do we ensure Data Trust?	Believing the accuracy of the data that is captured, transmitted, and stored is essential and will increase, based on the criticality of the data. There may be a need for multiple devices to collect the "same" data or other validation metrics to increase confidence.
☐	7.1.8 How do we ensure Processing Trust?	Having confidence, in the outcomes of analysis and our ability to come to the correct conclusions, is necessary before we can carry out actions. Determining the appropriate checks and balances will depend on the nature of our operating environment. In mission-critical environments, this may require multiple separate systems that must agree on a result before action is taken.

☒	Question	Why this matters
☐	7.1.9 Do our systems need to support real-time operations?	The degree of infrastructure resilience required for real-time industrial systems (e.g. a power station), is significantly different from, non-time critical or long-term data gathering (fencing on a farm, weather station). A similar point is made below concerning security.
☐	7.1.10 Do we have specific requirements for where data centres are located?	Part of the attraction for the "as-a-Service" model is that, the details of operations are taken care of by someone else, however, there may be legal, contractual or moral obligations to use "in country" services. Also, don't forget to check where the supplier stores data for reliability and disaster recovery purposes.
☐	7.1.11 Have our customers specified or set expectations regarding requirements for the location of data storage?	Organisations are becoming increasingly aware of the requirements for protecting data held by 3rd parties and are including these requirements in contract terms. Where data is stored on behalf of, or for customers, there may be an implied or possibly explicit responsibility for its security. Even if the customer is not currently aware of this situation, we can be sure they will raise it if something goes wrong (Consider US data in North Korea or Iranian data held in a US data centre.).
☐	7.1.12 Is our approach to customise or configure?	Customising an existing product results in a unique version, that will require dedicated and ongoing maintenance. Configuration uses parameters and settings to create a potentially unique combination of options, but still within the original product. It is critical to carefully assess the pros and cons of each approach and where, the true transformative business value exists.

☒	Question	Why this matters
☐	7.1.13 Have we assessed the technical debt[87] across the current systems and applications in our organisation?	When implementing systems, decisions taken to gain benefits in the short term, can lead to long term costs in areas such as support and flexibility. These decisions maybe entirely appropriate however, it is essential to have a clear understanding of this "technical debt" within the current systems so the impact on the digital transformation project can be assessed. This may relate to data migration, interoperability with new systems, long term support etc.
☐	7.1.14 How will the project handle technical debt with new systems?	The use of 3rd party "as a service" offerings has the benefit of shifting the responsibility for technical debt to them, however, this can also reduce the level of control and/or limit the ability to differentiate. There needs to be a model that balances the benefits of speed and short-term flexibility with the longer-term impact of technical debt. This "balance" is likely to vary across different system areas.
☐	7.1.15 Is a change in IT systems required to deliver the desired business process change?	The implementation of new systems can be a catalyst to drive new business processes, however, it is also possible that existing systems are just as capable of delivering the new processes There will still be training required to shift users from their current way of using the system, which may be less than the training costs and lost productivity incurred with new systems.

---

[87] https://en.wikipedia.org/wiki/Technical_debt

☒	Question	Why this matters
☐	7.1.16 What are the metrics to measure the success of the project?	There needs to be a framework identifying the overall end to end business metrics and identifying the technology metrics, including detail on expectations. This will enable the ability to continually assess the impact as the project progresses and mitigate risks, by making informed decisions and changes if necessary. There needs to be a framework that tracks the overall end to end business and technology metrics, that define the success of the digital transformation project. This will enable the ability to continually assess the impact of the project, as it progresses, to make informed decisions, to mitigate risks and make changes when, not if, necessary.
☐	7.1.17 How do we build growth into our infrastructure plans?	If the predictions/hype are true, then our growth will be exponential. There needs to be some sanity and thought put into how much data will be accumulated, and whether everything in the infrastructure can scale both locally and globally. This will help future proof the investment.
☐	7.1.18 Who is responsible for understanding the licensing terms of the various providers & suppliers?	Licensing can be complex with different pricing models based on various measures, e.g. users & devices. The variations in licensing models can have a fundamental impact on the economics of the project. Having a detailed understanding of licensing can help shape the way services are selected and deployed, from the outset, rather than getting a shock later.

☒	Question	Why this matters
☐	7.1.19 Have we considered the hidden/ additional costs of the new services in the cloud?	Data ingress/egress, storage, processing monitoring and actions all add to the costs of running business systems in the cloud. Having a detailed understanding of cloud services and how they are billed will help shape the way services are selected and deployed, from the design phase. This will reduce the risk of "Cloud Bill Shock" and spiralling unforeseen costs.
☐	7.1.20 What do we do with our existing systems?	Existing systems may no longer be fit for purpose and just need replacing, however, other options are available and may be appropriate. For example; when considering the migration of applications to the cloud, there are two popular frameworks: Gartner (2011) propose 5 ways[88] they can be migrated: • Rehost • Refactor • Revise • Rebuild • Replace Amazon Web Services (2016) have 6 options for migration[89]: • Rehost • Re-platform • Repurchase • Refactor / Re-architect • Retire • Retail Adopting a framework such as these, will provide a consistent approach.

---

[88] *https://www.gartner.com/newsroom/id/1684114*
[89] *https://aws.amazon.com/blogs/enterprise-strategy/6-strategies-for-migrating-applications-to-the-cloud/*

☒	Question	Why this matters
☐	7.1.21 What technology service platform do we need?	From deployment and management of systems and devices through to the visualisation of insights, and automated actions, the range of services required to deliver systems can be complex. Even starting small it is unlikely that we will develop these services ourselves. There are many platforms available and understanding our business strategy and organisational readiness will guide us. • Some platforms such as Microsoft Azure, Amazon AWS, Google Cloud and IBM SoftLayer and Bluemix, offer a building blocks approach. Their ecosystem of partners will use these blocks to build out industry vertical solutions. • Others such as GE and Hitachi have created tightly integrated solutions around their existing industrial offerings. • Companies with strong business rules engines such as Salesforce and ServiceNow can drive business actions • There are solutions aligned to specific industry verticals. • Start-ups offering independent end-to-end solutions are growing rapidly.
☐	7.1.22 Is this a chance to drive standardised processes?	Over time different areas of the business can implement various solutions to the same business process. This could be due to business acquisitions, department specific solutions, shadow IT etc. This can lead to inefficiencies, additional costs and a lack of flexibility (see technical debt above). There may be significant savings and enhanced business benefits if standardised processes can be implemented.

☒	Question	Why this matters
☐	7.1.23 What existing projects will be impacted?	A review of existing projects will help to understand their impact on the digital transformation program. Existing projects that are in flight may be difficult to change and their business cases may be impacted, positively or negatively. Some may integrate well and act as accelerators, for others there may be the difficult decision to cancel or limit the project for the longer term good.
☐	7.1.24 What are our business continuity processes (BCP) and disaster recovery (DR) requirements?	Things break. The nature and criticality of the environment will determine the level of BCP/DR investments. There needs to be a strategy based on business requirements which make it clear about how often recovery rehearsals are carried out, how much data the business can afford to lose (RPO – recovery point objective) and how quickly the data and services need to be recovered (RTO – recovery time objective), in the event of an outage or incident.
☐	7.1.25 Can our existing or proposed storage solution scale to our needs over time?	Storage is relatively low cost, but it is not free. Volumes can increase rapidly as the business grows and increases the retention period. There should be planning in place on how the storage solution scales over time and what the expected pricing will be.
☐	7.1.26 Do our customers require data segregation?	Some existing customer contracts may have clauses that require the business to store their data separate from others. Alternatively, this could also be a value-add offering.

X	Question	Why this matters
☐	7.1.27 Do we need access to 3rd party data to provide the required insights?	Project requirements may necessitate external data to deliver the insights the business is looking to gather. Validating the commercial and technical terms for accessing this data, and how regularly the data needs to be updated, may impact both costs and systems design.
☐	7.1.28 Will we be able to combine data from different sources to provide a single view?	Connecting data from new and old systems can be challenging. A lack of standards may result in data being captured and stored in varying formats. The odds are there will be a need for common "keys" that link different data sources together. Getting the data storage design right up front is important; however, having the flexibility to adapt and learn if requirements change is important as well. This is the area of Data Semantics[90].
☐	7.1.29 What data management obligations do we have?	The strategy and compliance framework must consider the laws, regulations, policies, and standards requirements, for each country in which; the data resides, services operate, or the clients resides. Clarity and understanding of how these are driven, by regulatory bodies or customer needs, is important. Although internally a business may be relaxed about who can see what, there are often clear legal requirements for retention and privacy, and these vary depending on the countries in which the business operates.

---

[90] *https://en.wikipedia.org/wiki/Semantic_data_model*

☒	Question	Why this matters
☐	7.1.30 What languages and currencies do we need to support?	Even if the current business operations are in a single geography, digital transformation is likely to open other markets. Whilst English, is understood in many markets, it is not universal. Even if a decision is made to support a single currency, there is still a decision about payment methods. Visa and Mastercard are obvious, but what about WeChat Pay, PayPal or even Bitcoin?

7.2 The Technical questions not to be scared to ask

In this section we could offer 100's of detailed technical questions that relate to digital transformation, however that is another book.

Rather, our goal is to share a selection of questions across multiple areas that we trust will provide insights into the issues that your technical teams will (should) be considering. We also hope that the "why this matters" column will help in breaking down the technical language barrier.

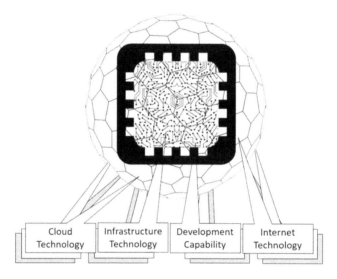

Figure 31 - The technical questions

Having a few questions in these areas could help to keep the technical team on their toes, with just one question being the catalyst for others to surface. For example, a simple question about how power will be provided to "Internet of Things" devices, should start the discussion about data volumes, transfer rates and ease of access, which will influence whether battery or mains power is appropriate and hence installation costs.

Who knows, these questions may even pique your own interest to dive deeper into the wonderful (IOHO) world of technology.

☒	Question	Why this matters
☐	7.2.1 Do we have sufficient capacity in our core network?	The move of services from the internal network (self-hosted), to external providers and supply chain partners, will shift the focus on bandwidth requirements from the existing internal high-speed LAN networks to external WAN network connections. Bandwidth that was suitable for the exchange of emails may buckle under the pressure of rich content (videos). Latency will also be a focus for real time applications (accounting). Depending on the physical location of an office, the network connection choices will vary. CBD locations will often have access to the high-speed Fibre services (1Gbps). Other locations may still be limited to 10-20Mbps.
☐	7.2.2 What will need to be upgraded in our network infrastructure?	With the increase in data volumes and external connections it is likely that routers and firewalls will need to be reviewed, for their ability to handle the increased requirements. This will not just be throughput/capacity but also in areas such as, security and network management.
☐	7.2.3 Will our remote users have sufficient bandwidth?	With more users working away from the office and an expectation of always on access, the requirements for internet access will significantly grow. Even a few years ago, contracts negotiated with network providers for 1GB/user of data, may have seemed plenty, however, today 10's of Gb is the norm and for power users, this may need to be considerably more.

☒	Question	Why this matters
☐	7.2.4 How will we monitor the quality of service across our internal network?	Networks can get very sophisticated and challenging to manage however, they are the backbone for communications across the business. It is important to be sure the network is proactively monitored to prevent issues and outages. What happens when the users of the SaaS accounting system get slow response, because other users are watching YouTube videos during their lunch break? What happens if the network slows down at 9am, when a new software update starts to be delivered to all the smart phones that have just connected to the Wi-Fi? Both monitoring and management will be required to identify where and why issues are occurring and then apply rules to ensure quality of service (QoS).
☐	7.2.5 How will we monitor the quality of service across external networks?	Monitoring internal networks, is within the direct control of the network team, however, performance issues with access to SaaS applications can also occur, because of issues with the external networks. This could be the networks of multiple telecom providers, or within the network at the data centre hosting the SaaS application. Poor performance can be a major blocker to end user acceptance of new systems. Tools that monitor performance and bottlenecks across these external networks, will allow the network team to proactively manage this critical area.
☐	7.2.6 How do we manage access to external services?	When most services were on the internal network, there was limited requirement for users to have external access. This often led to a logical approach of "all access is blocked unless specifically requested". As more external services are used this will increase the overhead of managing the control of external access.

☒	Question	Why this matters
☐	7.2.7 How will we manage access from external parties to services on our network?	With more remote users and increasing integration with supply chains, there will be a growing requirement to allow external parties to connect into systems on the core network. Opening this access creates security risks and needs to be managed. There are multiple technical solutions that can support this, but there will also be new processes that need to be put in place for example, some access may only be temporary, but what process is in place to ensure it is turned off?
☐	7.2.8 What is our approach for device provisioning and management?	In general, the more standardised the provisioning, build and manage, the cheaper and easier it is to automate and maintain. Managing devices that may, or may not, be connected to the core network, be online, belong to the company (BYOD) or even be accessed by a human, creates a wide range of challenges. What happens if a staff members personal device, which has company emails on it, is lost? What capability and rights are there to remotely wipe the device?
☐	7.2.9 What is our approach for application management on remote devices?	Managing applications and their data on remote devices, is a critical task for security and productivity purposes. Did you know that 12,000 laptops a week go missing at US airports[91]? Mobile Device Management (MDM) and Mobile Application management (MAM), are two similar approaches, but with a potentially very different experience for users. MAM can clear specific apps and their data e.g. Outlook, whereas MDM is a more scorched earth approach.

[91] http://www.dell.com/downloads/global/services/dell_lost_laptop_study.pdf

☒	Question	Why this matters
☐	7.2.10 How will we support our remote / external users?	Providing users with the ability to work anywhere can have a transformative impact, but if technology issues occur, are staff capable of self-support, or could self-support cause more problems? Staff working globally may need "follow the sun" support. Is this something you provide internally or should it be outsourced?
☐	7.2.11 Will user phones, PC's, laptops etc need to be upgraded?	The new services being deployed as part of the digital transformation program may have specific hardware and/or software requirements e.g. the latest version of Windows or Android, or the ability to run high quality graphics. Devices that have been happily running previous versions of software may no longer be fit for purpose.
☐	7.2.12 Do the systems/ applications we plan to keep need to be upgraded?	Existing applications that are being kept may still have to be upgraded. Upgrading a major line of business application will be a significant project on its own, even upgrading Microsoft Office, which may not appear to be too daunting, could introduce breaking changes e.g. macros, or require staff training to benefit from the new capabilities. In both cases the risks and effort are significantly increased if moving from a much older version.

☒	Question	Why this matters
☐	7.2.13 Are there new areas in our infrastructure that need redundancy?	As the technology infrastructure becomes more distributed, there will be new critical points of failure. When services were all in house, access to the internet was nice to have, but operations could still continue. Now, a failure with internet access can remove access to critical systems. If a user's home office setup failed, they could just come into the office, but what if the office has no spare capacity, or even no longer exists?
☐	7.2.14 How accurate do we make our disaster recovery rehearsals?	DR rehearsals have always been a compromise between completeness and minimising operational disruption. As services spread across multiple providers and interconnections within the supply chain grow, the ability to co-ordinate comprehensive end to end rehearsals becomes more challenging. The distribution of services could reduce the risk of disasters, with a failure of one SaaS provider, not directly impacting another. Careful segmentation of rehearsals may be required, to provide the appropriate level of confidence.
☐	7.2.15 What provision is available for remote users to work offline?	Some users may always be connected, (e.g. office workers), others such as executives and salespeople may not, and despite the wide availability of internet access, it cannot be guaranteed. If these users need access to certain services, even when "off-line", then solutions that offer a hybrid approach with a central "hosted" service and a local synchronised copy, will need to be considered.

☒	Question	Why this matters
☐	7.2.16 How do we manage synchronisation of user data and content updates from multiple devices?	Even where there are multiple copies of the same data, for example, to allow offline working, it is essential, for strong data management, that there is still a single "version of truth" copy. When a user can access data from multiple devices, or multiple users can access the data, there is the potential for synchronisation issues. An example of this is when an executive takes a copy of a spreadsheet to review while on the plane. When they land, they try to synchronise their copy, but somebody else has already saved an edited version.
☐	7.2.17 How will users manage access and proof of identity to multiple internal and external systems?	Maintaining a single complex password is a challenge for a user. Passwords for three applications or more becomes an issue for the business. Users will tend to write them down on post-its or other simple methods and paste them to their devices. Ways to prevent this need to be implemented. Some of the options include: <ul><li>Single-Sign on Apps</li><li>Biometric Authentication</li><li>Multifactor</li><li>OAuth (Open Authorization)</li><li>SAML (Security Assertion Mark-up Language)</li></ul>The risk of passwords being simplified or written down, is mitigated if the user only has to maintain one complexed password.

☒	Question	Why this matters
☐	7.2.18 How many environments will we need for each system?	Multiple environments are required to ensure that updates can be tested before they go into production, but how many will be needed, depends on the complexity and criticality of the system. For more complex systems this typically includes development, technical testing, user acceptance testing and production.
☐	7.2.19 What programming languages and code management approaches will we need to support?	Systems developed in house may be based on Microsoft standards. The use and customisation of a Salesforce instance will use a different approach. The more services being used, the higher the potential for a diversity of programming languages. Understanding what skills are required and how core each is to the business, will determine whether they are maintaining internally or outsourced.
☐	7.2.20 Do the "change freeze" periods of 3rd party suppliers match with ours?	No matter how well-planned changes to systems can go wrong. It is therefore common to have a "change freeze" policy during critical periods e.g. financial year end. If these change freeze periods are critical to your business, then understanding what, if any policies the potential 3rd party providers have, will be important in the selection process.

☒	Question	Why this matters
☐	7.2.21 Are we clear about our data centre requirements?	The requirements of the business are key to the decision-making process. There may be regulatory or contractual requirements that mean the data centre must be in country, meet a certain infrastructure design level (tier 1 to 4[92]), or support specific certifications (ISO 27001, HIPAA etc). Some data centres will only provide services on their own hardware. Others will provide the racks, power and communications and allow the relocation of existing servers.
☐	7.2.22 Do we need a hybrid approach to meet our data centre requirements?	The data centre requirements for one area of the business may require sophisticated, expensive data centre capability. Other areas may be straight forward. Other systems may be expensive or too risky to move from their current infrastructure. There are benefits of a common solution approach, however, a cost/benefit analysis may make a hybrid approach more appropriate. • In-house • Local service provider • Private cloud Public/hyperscale cloud etc

---

[92] https://www.webopedia.com/TERM/D/data_center_tiers.html

☒	Question	Why this matters
☐	7.2.23 How will we manage resource utilisation across our data centre(s)?	The "load" placed on infrastructure varies with time. This could be as simple as following the working day (9 to 5), however, it is likely that there will be spikes due to specific events. Some of these such as financial year end, or Christmas shopping may be predictable, others may not (Kim Kardashian is seen wearing a dress and the designers web site traffic increases 1000%). Monitoring these loads and responding appropriately, ideally an automated process is critical to maintaining a great user experience, whether for internal staff or customers.
☐	7.2.24 What integration will be required between existing, temporary and new systems?	Systems and services that are going to be retained may need to be integrated with new systems while, other systems may only be kept on a temporary basis, but still need points of integration, to support a migration process. Depending on whether there are existing, well documented interfaces, OR these need to be coded from scratch, or existing ones need to be customised, can significantly change costs and complexity.
☐	7.2.25 What data will need to be migrated to new systems?	Even though systems are being replaced the data they hold is likely to still hold significant value. In some cases, it may be a compliance requirement to retain the data; in others it may be the history of customer relationships or internal process documentation and IP, that would be lost if not migrated. A good planning position is to assume, that data migration will be more complex than originally envisioned, and that critical data will be discovered at the last minute.

☒	Question	Why this matters
☐	7.2.26 How long will it take to migrate data?	The physical time it takes to move data can often come as a surprise in the migration process. As data volumes have exploded it is no longer unusual, even for small companies, to have 100's of terabytes or even petabytes of data[93]. Even with a high-speed internet connection (say 100Mbps) just 1 terabyte (8,000,000,000,000 bits) would take at least 24 hours to transfer (and this assumes theoretically perfect transfer rates). This is why many hosting companies offer physical migration services, where data is loaded onto hard drives and then shipped by courier. E.g. Amazon Snowball[94]
☐	7.2.27 Is there an opportunity to clean up and/or de-duplicate data before migration?	There are many reasons why data ends up being duplicated. It could be that the same customer has been added to the CRM system multiple times with slightly different spellings, or copies of documents, such as excel spreadsheets or design drawings are saved to multiple computers. Whatever the reason, duplication happens, and it can have a significant impact, increasing the data storage and backup requirements, creating processing confusion, with same customer but multiple names etc. The migration of data from one system to another provides a great opportunity to clean up data, just like moving house, it is amazing how much can be cleared out!!

---

[93] *https://en.wikipedia.org/wiki/Orders_of_magnitude_(data)*
[94] *https://aws.amazon.com/snowball/*

☒	Question	Why this matters
☐	7.2.28 What are our plans for managing growth in data volume?	In 2016, it was claimed that "More data will be created in 2017 than the previous 5,000 years of humanity"[95]. No matter what the source is, rich content such as video, data from millions of IoT devices or multimedia, data volumes are growing at exponential rates. A clear data management policy will help to clarify what data should be kept and for how long, whether the data needs to be available in real time or can be "restored" from long term backups etc. One thing that should be assumed is that there will be more data than was planned for.
☐	7.2.29 What is our design approach for edge vs core processing and data storage?	Vast amounts of data will be captured by devices at the "edge" of our networks. Should all of this data be transferred to a central location and processed there, or would localised processing reduce network volumes and allow actions even if offline? The answers will depend on the business case. For example, if a temperature probe captures data every 10 seconds, then the business rule could be to send data and trigger a local action, only if the temperature is above a certain level. If the goal is to identify trends that lead to overheating then the decision to carry out an action may be carried out locally, all data is still sent to central storage.
☐	7.2.30 How will power be provided to our Internet of Things devices?	Providing power to where an IoT device is deployed can create cost barriers such as approvals, electricians, cabling etc. Battery powered IoT devices are more convenient to deploy but bring compromises such as, minimizing the time they are active.

---

[95] *https://appdevelopermagazine.com/more-data-will-be-created-in-2017-than-the-previous-5,000-years-of-humanity-/*

☒	Question	Why this matters
☐	7.2.31 What type of network connection do we need for remote/IoT devices?	The growth of "non-user" devices connected to networks (aka IoT), should raise questions about the type connectivity required. Networks such as 4G and 5G offer high speed, high bandwidth capability, however, they are relatively short range and have higher power requirements. Networks such as, LoRaWAN and Sigfox ,offer long range and low power but have limited bandwidth. Real time video monitoring of a door, will have different requirements to a simple Open/Closed message. Understanding the real requirements can fundamentally change the speed and cost of roll out.
☐	7.2.32 How will we manage thousands or millions of Internet of Things devices?	Managing 100's of PC's is complex. Managing thousands or millions of IoT devices that are remote, with potentially limited processing capability, will be impossible if not planned for. The level of management will depend on the criticality of the devices. A sensor on a fence can fail with limited consequences, a sensor in a nuclear power station is another matter. Planning also needs to include the scalability of systems that receive messages from IoT devices; for example, a ticketing system may start to receive 1000's of alerts and have to determine if work orders need to be raised.
☐	7.2.33 Do we have sufficient data points to support a digital twins[96] solution?	The number of data points required to accurately mirror a real-world environment, into a digital copy, will vary depending on its complexity. Adding additional sensors may require time consuming actions e.g. the shut-down of parts of an oil refinery.

---

[96] https://en.wikipedia.org/wiki/Digital_twin

☒	Question	Why this matters
☐	7.2.34 Would a blockchain solution provide sufficient benefits to be an alternative to a traditional database approach?	There is a lot of hype around blockchain and plenty of headlines about crypto currencies. There are use cases where, the distribute ledger approach will have transformative value, however, it does come with costs, for example, in performance. It may be that a "boring" old fashioned SQL database solution can offer an equally capable, or better, solution with significantly less risk.
☐	7.2.35 Are our training materials stored in a way that would support an augmented/ virtual reality offering?	Augmented reality offers great opportunities in the area of training, to realise this, training materials, company knowledge, IP etc needs to be in a digital format. This could be a case of finding where existing digital copies are stored, however, it could require the capture of knowledge within experts' heads.
☐	7.2.36 What processes in our business would be significantly improved through robotic workforce automation (bots)?	There are many, typically repetitive and predicable, processes that are handled manually within businesses. These processes are ripe for automation. There can be social concerns, "the robots are coming", however the more positive view is that skilled humans will be freed up to do more valuable activities. A key to achieving the optimal benefits is to decide if existing processes should be automated as-is, or whether the whole process can be re-thought.

☒	Question	Why this matters
☐	7.2.37 Do we have sufficient data to "train" our machine learning and AI plans?	This is a "how long is a piece of string" question, the answer will depend on the complexity of the problem, the associated learning algorithms and will almost certainly be more than initially envisaged. The data required may already exist within the business, or be relatively easy to acquire from external sources, it is also likely that there will need to be a conscious effort to acquire new data to fill the current gaps.

7.3 Cyber Security, Security & Privacy

Digital Transformation and change introduce new security and privacy risks and/or bring into sharp relief existing ones that have been missed or ignored. Differing industries also have different exposures and priorities

- The floor plan of a shared office space carries less risk if stolen than the detailed schematics of a nuclear power station.
- The name and email address of a CEO at a publicly traded company, has less privacy concerns if shared than the details of patients at a hospital.

Therefore, the posture in understanding and mitigating these risks needs to be specifically tailored to the business type and market. Privacy is the outcome, security is one of the tools.

Figure 32 - Cyber security, security and privacy

There is legislation in the works[97] which makes the cyber security of an organisation a board responsibility. As a member of a board, ignorance does not preclude you from prosecution. [98]

Although legislation is supposed to create clarification, the emerging nature of digital transformation means that legislation is immature or in some cases does not exist. The global nature of

---

[97] *https://asic.gov.au/regulatory-resources/corporate-governance/corporate-governance-articles/cyber-security-and-directors/*

[98] *https://www.gtlaw.com.au/insights/fishing-dynamite/gathering-storm-%E2%80%93-directors%E2%80%99-duties-use-misuse-data*

digital transformation also introduces multiple layers of complexity and compliance. This lack of clarity can create great business opportunities, but also potential conflicts and a risk of being seen as "not doing the right thing". This all leads to a greater reliance on strong business ethics.

In this, our final section we have captured our experiences to help you navigate this complex area

(n.b. please see pervious caveat in the legal section – we are not lawyers, please do your own due diligence)

> The bottom line is, there is no way to guarantee that there will not be a data breach or other attack on your systems, the organisation needs to be seen to have a strategy and plan in place, to be able to detect it, mitigate the damage and recover from it.

[X]	Question	Why this matters
☐	7.3.1 What policies have been developed and ratified by our board relating to security?	If there are security policies in place within the organisation, is the board aware of them and have they been tested to make sure they are relevant? • Cyber • Data • User What others are required?
☐	7.3.2 How does Digital security fit into our digital strategy?	There are several security issues to address. However, there needs to be a security strategy developed as part of our digital strategy. To try to implement security after the fact can be very difficult and costly. The philosophy of "Secure by Design" is gaining more momentum as the number of security failures and data breaches grow.
☐	7.3.3 What is the position of our local company regulators to cyber threats?	Organisations charged with the oversight of corporate governance are making increasingly clear signs that, they are monitoring businesses for their posture towards cyber threats, as an example, ASIC in Australia state[99], "We will focus on serious breaches where these indicate failure by corporations to respond appropriately to the threat of malicious cyber activity."
☐	7.3.4 Have we completed a systems risk analysis from a security perspective?	Having a detailed understanding of the risks from a security perspective, (likelihood and impact) associated with a loss or breach of service, data or any other areas of consideration will assist in justifying the implementation of appropriate mitigation strategies within the infrastructure.

---

[99] *http://asic.gov.au/about-asic/asic-investigations-and-enforcement/asic-enforcement-outcomes/*

☒	Question	Why this matters
☐	7.3.5 Do we have an impact classification model for data that we collect and store?	Not all data is born equal, some are designed to be in the public domain, and some will have a significant impact if shared. Not understanding this can lead to over or under engineering and poorly directed investment. Consideration for the data both in isolation, and when combined with other data, needs to be addressed. Some other drivers will be legislation, reputational risks and social expectations.
☐	7.3.6 Are we subject to data retention requirements?	There may be a legal obligation to retain data captured for a specified period, or conversely require its deletion. Understanding how the data is handled at the end of any retention period, and whether there is a need to have data discovery capabilities (e.g. GDPR), will clarify any potential risks and liability.
☐	7.3.7 Does our data need to be encrypted?	The simple answer could be yes, it is important to be clear about where encryption occurs to minimise any exposure points in the infrastructure. If local to the device then more processing power and storage may be required at an extra cost, and if needed, be clear about responsibilities for the maintenance of the encryption keys (a non-trivial task).
☐	7.3.8 Does the business have a strategy to deal with Data theft?	Organisations need to have strategies in place to deal with data theft. Social and formal legislative pressure means that this cannot be an after-thought; it needs to be part of the security strategy.

☒	Question	Why this matters
☐	7.3.9 Does the business have a strategy to deal with Network breaches?	Does the organisation have strategies and systems in place to detect and deal with hacking of the network? With the proliferation of hacking and malware, the organisation should operate under the assumption it has been hacked/breached. This reduces the risk of losses in the event of an actual breach, which is not identified right away.
☐	7.3.10 What is the business posture towards paying to recover from Ransomware attacks?	Hopefully it will not happen (although plan that it will), and if it does then you have backups and plans that will allow you to recover. Paying the cyber-criminals may be the only option if you want to recover the data. Thinking ahead of time about the moral and commercial issues involved, will make decision making quicker in the event of a disaster.
☐	7.3.11 What standards have our external partners implemented relating to data protections?	With an increasingly connected supply chain it is likely that suppliers, partners etc will have copies of potentially sensitive data. Understanding how to verify and validate the standards they are implementing for backup, recovery, business continuity, and security of data could be important for our own compliance requirements.
☐	7.3.12 Who is responsible for considering new or emerging security threats?	New threats are occurring on an ongoing basis and existing threats are being amplified. These need to be considered in the context of: • Security Differentiators – the new threats unique to emerging systems & Technologies (e.g. IoT) Security Multipliers – the enhancement of risks due to the volume of devices.

☒	Question	Why this matters
☐	7.3.13 What level of security or encryption will be required for devices?	If a device (laptop, phone etc) is lost or stolen, either by accident or maliciously, then what would be the business impact? This will vary based on the type of data exposed (see 7.3.5 "impact classification model") and the impact will determine the effort expended to protect it.
☐	7.3.14 Has the business implemented any standards relating to the protection of intellectual property?	Many new ideas and processes are likely to be created during a transformation process. People may be hired because of the skills and IP they bring with them. Being clear about who owns this IP and, as far as possible, capturing it in a structured/documented way, may be important in ensuring the ongoing activities of the business.
☐	7.3.15 What policies and processes are in place relating to the privacy of personally identifiable data?	Privacy is a hot topic in general and recent legislation around the world has made the protection of personally identifiable data even more critical. Being clear about what data is held and where for example, a complete copy of the customer database, extracted to a spreadsheet, and saved to the laptop of a junior member of the marketing team, for use on a marketing communications campaign, will be critical to understanding what exposures and corporate risk may exist. This in turn will inform the effort expended to protect it in the first place and then detect and notify in the event of loss.
☐	7.3.16 What policies and processes do we have in place to allow for discovery and deletion of personally identifiable data?	Legislation such as GDPR allows for discovery and data requests. Identifying data within your data stores in advance and having policies to respond will reduce disruption and effort, as well as speeding up the process of being compliant. Many software vendors are adding capabilities into their systems to assist in "tagging" personal data.

[X]	Question	Why this matters
☐	7.3.17 Who owns the data that we collect?	When we collect data either directly or indirectly, have we clarified whether we have the rights to own the data and if so, have we informed the originator of our assumption of ownership?
☐	7.3.18 Has the business implemented any standards relating to accessing internal systems?	In many cases it is not the level of access a staff member has in one area of the business that creates an exposure, but rather their combined access e.g. raising expenditure requests in their current marketing role and then using authority from their time in accounts to approve the request. The digital transformation process, will introduce changes in systems and organisational structure, which could, if not monitored, create these "combined authority" exposures.
☐	7.3.19 Do we have a segregation of responsibilities for monitoring and operating?	Despite best efforts, self-regulation often falls short of expectations. The pressures on operational activities to "get stuff done" means that "oversight", can take a poor back seat. New roles such as Chief Security Officer are intended to offer a separation between the operators and the people providing oversight. If nobody is watching AND taking actions, then the best systems in the world cannot protect us. Be clear about who is responsible for monitoring security.
☐	7.3.20 Do we create legal or ethical exposures when we aggregate data from multiple sources?	Data gathered may have limited exposure in isolation, when combined with other data, more significant exposures to security and privacy may occur. This may become increasingly relevant with machine learning and AI projects.

☒	Question	Why this matters
☐	7.3.21 Are there any data requirements our customer or suppliers would require?	Certain customers, suppliers or even governments may impose extended requirements on the business if we wish to trade with them. Achieving compliance with their requirements may create a competitive edge OR it may change the cost effectiveness of the relationship
☐	7.3.22 Have we considered using "white hat[100]" services to check our readiness for cyber threats?	White hat is the term used to refer to an ethical computer hacker, or a computer security expert. The growth of cybercrime has seen a corresponding growth in white hat services. These include penetration testing (trying to break into the network), sending emails which mimic those with malware attached and having training programs to educate those who clicked on the link etc.

---

[100] https://en.wikipedia.org/wiki/White_hat_(computer_security)

Chapter

Final Word

A conclusion is the place where you got tired of thinking.

Albert Bloch (American Artist, 1882 – 1961)

W E leave you with a simple thought that is definitely not new, but we trust that it will be motivational.

Figure 33 - The winds of change and opportunity

When the winds of change blow, some people build walls, others build windmills[101].

Do you want to someone trying to build walls to block change, or someone who builds windmills to harness the power of change and the opportunities it can bring?

---

[101] Chinese proverb

List of Figures

Getting Involved

The Smart Questions community

There may be questions that we should have asked but didn't. Or specific questions which may be relevant to your situation, but not everyone in general. Go to the website for the book and post the questions. You never know, they may make it into the next edition of the book. That is a key part of the Smart Questions Philosophy.

Send us your feedback

We love feedback. We prefer great reviews, but we'll accept anything that helps take the ideas further. We welcome your comments on this book.

We'd prefer email, as it's easy to answer and saves trees. If the ideas worked for you, we'd love to hear your success stories. Maybe we could turn them into 'Talking Heads'-style video or audio interviews on our website, so others can learn from you. That's one of the reasons why we wrote this book. So, talk to us.

feedback@smart-questions.com

Got a book you need to write?

Maybe you are a domain expert with knowledge locked up inside you. You'd love to share it and there are people out there desperate for your insights. But you don't think you are an author and don't know where to start. Making it easy for you to write a book is part of the Smart Questions Philosophy.

Let us know about your book idea, and let's see if we can help you get your name in print.

potentialauthor@Smart-Questions.com

Notes pages

We hope that this book has inspired you and that you have already scribbled your thoughts all over it. However, if you have ideas that need a little more space then please use these notes pages.

www.ingramcontent.com/pod-product-compliance
Lightning Source LLC
LaVergne TN
LVHW012331060326
832902LV00011B/1823